The Prop

SERIES EDITORS:
Erika Balsom (King's College London)
and **Genevieve Yue** (The New School)

"This new series of small-format books focused on cinematic motifs, themes, and devices represents something new and exciting in English-language writing on film" —**Dennis Lim, Artistic Director, New York Film Festival**

"Featuring some of the field's most exciting scholars and critics, Cutaways is a welcome addition to film writing. The series promises to expand the ways cinema is conceived, consumed, and received, in ways that parallel the contemporary situation of cinema." —**Sarah Keller, author of *Anxious Cinephilia: Pleasure and Peril at the Movies***

Cutaways is a series of pocket-sized books by and for movie lovers. Each volume offers a journey through the history of cinema guided by a single motif or formal device. Featuring original writing by film scholars and critics, the books create a space for intellectually engaged and broadly accessible cinephilia.

The Prop

Elena Gorfinkel and John David Rhodes

FORDHAM UNIVERSITY PRESS   NEW YORK   2025

Copyright © 2025 Fordham University Press

All rights reserved. No part of this publication may be reproduced, stored in a retrieval system, or transmitted in any form or by any means—electronic, mechanical, photocopy, recording, or any other—except for brief quotations in printed reviews, without the prior permission of the publisher.

Fordham University Press has no responsibility for the persistence or accuracy of URLs for external or third-party Internet websites referred to in this publication and does not guarantee that any content on such websites is, or will remain, accurate or appropriate.

Fordham University Press also publishes its books in a variety of electronic formats. Some content that appears in print may not be available in electronic books.

Visit us online at www.fordhampress.com.

Library of Congress Cataloging-in-Publication Data available online at https://catalog.loc.gov.

Printed in the United States of America
27 26 25   5 4 3 2 1
First edition

Contents

1. A Strand of Rope 1

2. Reading for the Prop 13

3. Prop Value 32

4. Realism, or the Prop's Thereness 53

5. The Prop and the Performer 80

6. Modalities of the Prop beyond the Studio 95

Coda: Golden Rain Tree 115

Theses on the Prop 119

Acknowledgments 125

Notes 127

List of Figures 137

Index 139

The Prop

1
A Strand of Rope

The prop is the object of inconsequential conspicuousness and conspicuous inconsequence. For cinema to take place, typically speaking, there must be a camera that records and something before it. What is before the camera—the pro-filmic—can be any of three entities, or these entities in any combination: a body (human or animal); space (the natural world, real places edified by humans, the self-enclosure of the film set); things themselves (objects: large and small, organic and inorganic, bought or fabricated, etc.). We have histories and theories of the actor's body in cinema, of its appearance before and performance for the camera, of its capturing by the camera, of its preservation and archiving by and on the filmstrip. We also have histories and theories of how space and place have been captured, harnessed, narrativized by cinema. But oddly, film theory and history tell us very little—or so it would seem at first glance—about that third category, the category of objects, or, as we call them in the jargon of film production, props.

Strangely, however, although there is no unified discourse that constitutes a theory of the prop per se, a proper theory

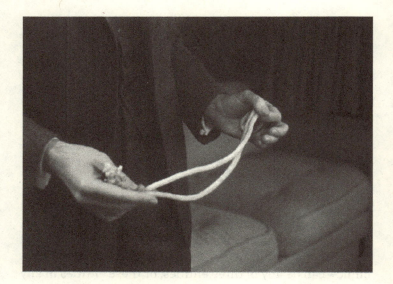

of the prop, the prop pops up, over and over again, in film theory, early, classical, and late. Its appearance in theory often has about it the happenstance-ness of an actual prop's appearance in a film. It is ready to hand, and, once handled, makes theory possible.

Witness the claims made for the prop (the object in film) by André Bazin in his essay "Theater and Cinema, Part Two," in a section titled "Behind the Décor":

> The human being is all-important in the theater. The drama on the screen can exist without actors. A banging door, a leaf in the wind, waves beating on the shore can heighten the dramatic effect. Some film masterpieces use man only as an accessory, like an extra, or in counterpoint

to nature which is the true leading character. ... As Jean-Paul Sartre, I think it was, said, in the theater the drama proceeds from the actor, in the cinema it goes from the decor to man. This reversal of the dramatic flow is of decisive importance. It is bound up with the very essence of the *mise-en-scène*. One must see here one of the consequences of photographic realism. Obviously, if the cinema makes use of nature it is because it is able to. The camera puts at the disposal of the director all the resources of the telescope and the microscope. The last strand of a rope about to snap or an entire army making an assault on a hill are within our reach.[1]

Bazin's use of the term "decor" clearly covers a wide stretch of terrain: the architecture of human habitation (the banging door), the tiniest unit of the natural world (the leaf), and terrain itself (the ocean and its beating waves). Of these, perhaps only the door would occur to us as a likely candidate for slotting into the category of the prop, which we tend to think of as something quite small, manageable or able to be manipulated by human hands—portable, existing in scale in some relation to the human body. The bleeding of the distinctions among doors and leaves and the ocean is explained by a sentence that seems merely an aside, but carries with it an enormous charge: "Obviously, if the cinema makes use of nature it is because it is able to." In other words, cinema's capacity for indexing the world means that it turns everything in the world into just another thing that it can index and, perhaps, put to further use in the telling of a story, the narrativization of existence. The world is the cinema's prop. Some things in the world seem closer to what we might think of as props, but "the consequences of photographic realism" render everything in the world susceptible to becoming a prop for the cinema. A "strand of rope" or "an entire army": Cinema makes use—in essence, makes props—of them both. Bazin licenses us to approach the prop as kernel, a condensation of the world's availability to the cinema, and cinema's endless instrumental exploitation of this availability.

This little book—a book whose scale is commensurate with the minor status of the prop itself—explores the possibilities of thinking cinema through the prop, perhaps the smallest unit of cinematic representation and signification.[2] We will be less than systematic. In fact, we may even at times be "arbitrary and aberrant." These are words used by Pier Paolo Pasolini in describing the cinema's predicament of having no language to rely on, and therefore, of having to invent itself via the camera's encounter with the things of the world.[3]

What if we stayed close to a film in order to explore some of what we are interested in here? What if we took into consideration, as an arbitrary starting place, a film about a strand of rope, about the aftermath of a murder, one undertaken with a strand of rope? And what if that film took its title from that bit of rope—were named, in other words, after its most significant prop?

Rope (1948) was Alfred Hitchcock's first color film and one that he described as "a stunt."[4] Hitchcock refers, of course, to the fact that the film, notoriously, is (or proposes itself to be) made up of a single long take. The subject of the film was adapted directly from an eponymous stage play by Patrick Hamilton. As a loose re-telling of the Leopold-Loeb murders, the film focuses on the murder of David (Dick Hogan, in a role that lasts only a few seconds) by two young men, Brandon (John Dall) and Philip (Farley Granger). It is set entirely in Brandon's stylishly luxurious New York City penthouse apartment. Brandon and Philip hide David's body in a large chest and then serve dinner to a party of guests that includes David's parents, his fiancée, and Rupert (James Stewart), who taught Brandon and Philip at prep school. Rupert slowly begins to unravel the secret that his former students are hiding, discovers the body, and manages to disarm them, and alert the police (by firing a gun into the sky out the window of the penthouse).

Although the film's events are acted out in what seems like real time, these are not, of course, actually recorded in one single take (an impossible feat for a movie of this length shot on film), but rather a series of several long takes joined together by edits that are masked or hidden by complicated cinematic choreography.[5] The camera's elegant parsing and pursuit of the narrative action also depended on the deft movement of movable props, manipulated by hands and bodies of stagehands unseen.

In order to make this whole set of operations possible, rigorous advanced planning was required: Furniture had to be placed on wheels, and a modest army of "stagehands" (Hitchcock's term)[6] stood by to manipulate this small, self-enclosed universe of movable property. The extraordinary labor required to produce the film needed to be simultaneously effaced. The film's unfolding could be understood as the product of a threefold labor process: (1) the labor of the actors; (2) the labor of the cinematographer; and (3) the labor of the stagehands, which was essentially a labor of prop management.[7]

Rope is, as its title suggests, a film about props—about things that are used to do things. We can assert this with confidence because the dinner party that Brandon throws is itself a performance, one that runs almost as long as the film itself, one that is predicated on a careful but not careful enough management of the props of domesticity and upper-middle-class entertaining. Because everyone in the film is stuck on the set that is Brandon's apartment, this location forces the actors into a more concentratedly busy engagement with the mise-en-scène. And it simultaneously forces our awareness of the same.[8] The film is a prolonged exercise in foregrounding what the industry calls "business": the actors' (play-acted) mindful or mindless, conscious or unconscious manipulation of and fidgeting with objects in the mise-en-scène.[9] Brandon attempts to set right what D. A. Miller calls a "canted candle"; cigarettes are endlessly lit and smoked; Philip returns repeatedly to play the piano; drinks are poured; food is served and eaten; and on and on. The fidgeting with props is what sustains the illusion of the film's natural bodying forth of its narrative contents, but worrying props is a worrisome activity, and it will be Rupert's too close inspection of one prop in particular that will help him solve the crime. This prop is David's monogrammed hat, mistakenly handed to Rupert by his housekeeper Mrs. Wilson (Edith Evanson); the presence of the hat reveals that David must have been in the apartment earlier, and, of course, is still there, in the chest in the living room, dead.

Brandon confuses his guests by the decision to have the buffet supper served on the chest, inside of which is David's corpse. He explains the oddity of moving the buffet onto this insufficient surface as necessitated by his desire to display on the dining table a collection of rare books that he hopes to sell to David's father (the sale another pretext for this elaborately staged party). His guests remain a little puzzled by his explanation. At one point we see a bit of the rope used to strangle David hanging dangerously out of the chest. Brandon—in his dizzying performance as writer, director, actor, and property manager—catches and corrects this continuity error.

The prop threatens to give the game away, in the same way that a continuity error involving a prop reminds us that a film is not real, that human labor has produced it, and that human labor is prone to error. Brandon is the prop master, he who tests the bounds of the legibility of the crime, as well as the bounds of an idea that arbitrates which humans have value and which can be tossed and trussed like things. Brandon must carry off his management of props for his dinner party to have its intended effect, just as Hitchcock (and his actors and production crew) must carry off the management of props for *Rope* to carry itself off. Of course, *Rope* carrying itself off means two things at once: (1) the film must offer us effortless access to its fictional world; and (2) it must convince those of us who are watching it precisely to see if it can pull off the virtuosic "stunt" of having managed to do so (again, apparently, effortlessly). The proper functioning and management of props is key to both of these stories—the story that is being represented and the story of the mounting of that representation. The prop, in *Rope* and in any fiction film, is invisible visibility: the stuff that populates the fictional world and makes it seem like *the* world. But as happens at several moments in *Rope*, the prop also functions to declare its visibility, as well as its sensual concreteness. "Do (not) look at me!" is the line delivered mutely by every prop, over and over.

We could say that, in *Rope*, the props become accessories to the crime in a double sense: They both accessorize the constrained space within which the corpse-prop's posthumous drama unfolds, and they saturate the actions of the murderers with meaning. Cigarettes and glasses, books and ropes, candlesticks and hats: All are accessories, in several senses, and as accessories to the crime, all are employed as ornaments of human culpability.

Rope is also a film of bodies. And props—in this film or in any other—will also presuppose the question of embodiment. The body is inherently bound up in the prop's facture and function. The body is onscreen but unseen; it props up the film's latent preoccupation with the dread of an inevitable, deferred revelation. Meanwhile the living bodies of the murderers variously finesse and fumble their efforts to conceal their crime—to test the concealment of the murder they have committed, which is itself the film's constitutive, founding action.

There is a dead body in a wooden chest hidden inside the frame, framed by the camera's constantly reframing movements. The fictional dead body becomes a prop by virtue of its invisible propping up of the narrative. The body anchors the narrative, goads its forward movement. The dead body is the sacrificial object that allows us to enter the space of the fiction, into the implications of the body's (un)becoming, by its having just been made dead, made into a thing, by way of being strangled with a thing, the eponymous rope. The process by which the human person comes to occupy the status of thing—that is to say, of prop (albeit an invisible one)—occurs almost invisibly, as the film begins. The film's duration preoccupies itself with managing this thing, which is placed inside another thing. Never visible, but always present, the dead body imbues the proceedings with the fetid air of fatality. But also, with irony. The dead body in a chest may be an ideal encapsulation of the tension between human and non-human that any prop animates and energizes.

Has the film's narrative stopped before it has begun? What Hitchcock shows us in *Rope* is that as much as cinematic narrative needs bodies, location, and light, it also requires things, and specifically *props* in order to arrange itself, to come into existence, to be. Hitchcock's fabled device of the "MacGuffin" should be recalled here. The MacGuffin is a device that catalyzes the plot but is ultimately peripheral to the film's actual interest. In *Notorious* (1946), for instance, the MacGuffin is, in Hitchcock's words, "concrete and visual: a sample of uranium concealed in a wine bottle."[10] In *Rope*, instead, we find the prop in some kind of oblique relation to Hitchcock's use of the MacGuffin. The dead body in the chest, the prop inside a prop, something we can't see hidden inside something we can: the dead body inside the chest which gives the film its narrative trajectory. Unlike some MacGuffins, we know what it is, yet there is an inverse anxiety that tilts in the direction of an anticipation—a perverse hope perhaps?—that Brandon and Philip might get away with it all. Will this prop—this chest, which, we might remind ourselves, has been pressed into serving double duty as an ad hoc buffet table, a prop twice over in other words—be recognized as the container of another thing that will detonate the fiction's climax and hasten it toward its immediate denouement, or will it merely recede into the scenery as just another wooden chest, a vessel for the always unremarkable and invisible unknown?

Constrained by a theatrical pretext that organizes narrative design, the set of *Rope* becomes a stage for the harnessing, channeling, and reconfiguration of props. Props circulate and accumulate in the apartment; they become networks in a web of deception, literally concealing from view the corpse that the spectator knows is right there. When discussing the murder, how it felt to still a body's rhythms, Brandon and Phillip conduct their heady conversation while popping open a champagne bottle. This minor operation, the liquid's bubbly effervescence, the delicacy with which a fragile glass must be held—all of these gestures and qualities suddenly draw a contrast with the force needed to strangle a human, to block the passage of air, to make someone alive into some *thing*, dead.

Hands manipulate props, grapple with them. Philip, a guilty hysteric, the less resolute of the two assassins, signals his slow giving way, his giving away of the game by crushing a champagne coupe in his hand when another guest, Mrs. Atwater (Constance Collier), mistakes him for David. The delicate glassware breaks, and the resulting blood is a displaced signifier of the violated body boxed up just a few feet away. Moments later, when Mrs. Atwater asks to read Philip's palm, his hand is miraculously unharmed and unbloodied.[11] Philip is a concert pianist; to calm his nerves he heads to the piano to play some Poulenc. Hands hold props and hands play pianos: Linked to the champagne glass by the contiguity of the hand that handles them both, the piano, which we might have thought too big to be considered a prop—is it not the subset of a more cumbersome category, like "set design" or decor?—is thoroughly remanded to propness. A vulnerability to being manipulated is something all props share. And props, in turn, are useful in manipulating the spectator into believing that this world exists, or at least in manipulating them into being interested enough in the fiction to sit still until the credits roll.[12]

If the hysterical criminal displaces his guilt onto the props he manipulates, we should note that props themselves are hysterical, or participate in the phenomenology of hysteria. They can be evidence, symptoms, symbols. They stand in for what cannot be said; they point to what cannot be explained. Even when at their most normative—the sofas and chairs and bric-a-brac that might denote a middle-class family home in, let's say, a Hollywood film like *There's Always Tomorrow* (Douglas Sirk, 1955)—the props' practice of standing there on the set is a standing in for a general idea of what a family home might look like. One fictional house might tilt more Colonial Revival, perhaps, while another film's living room might skew more midcentury modern, but the general function of the prop's summoning of generality is the same.[13] Brandon's apartment, in its wonderful plenitude of exquisitely curated objects, perhaps reads as "New York," or more narrowly as belonging to a "confirmed bachelor." The props that make up his apartment speak words that cannot be spoken, just as they conceal bodies that cannot be seen. (The chest hides David's body, but the apartment's décor offers camouflage to Brandon and Philip's unspeakable relationship, which, like the prop, remains visibly invisible.) They are tacitly faggy in their voluble, knowing muteness. Props are types, stereotypes, and as such, they compress and condense information, even while they clutter the set with their particularities, which are both real and totally bogus.

Rope has served, in a sense, as a prop for us: Perhaps too conveniently it models and performs so many of the possibilities for thinking through the prop, for subjecting it to analysis that will be as critical as it is fetishistic. As a hysterical subject, the prop speaks (again, always mutely) in many languages and in many conflicting registers. It is the point of utterance for ideas and concepts, large and small. To chart and describe some of these larger concerns is what we turn to now.

2
Reading for the Prop

In *Notes on the Cinematographer,* his acerbically epigrammatic compilation of reflections that amounts to an *ars poetica*, perhaps even to a theory of film, Robert Bresson remarks: "Make the objects look as if they want to be there."[1] Bresson asks us to take seriously objects that have been placed before the camera, or to take seriously the manner in which his "cinematographer" might do so. The statement admits that film is artifice (note: "make"), expresses an interest in the things in the world that the camera might be trained to capture, and flirts with a kind of personification, but nonetheless affirms the englobing of such activities inside fictionalization and narrativization (the "as if," familiar to us from Kant's suggestion that a work of art must act on us (its beholders) "as if it were a mere product of nature.")[2]

Bresson does not employ the word "prop," but we take the "objects" he refers to as examples of what we might call "props." Famously, in his own ascetic practice Bresson displaced the notion of the "actor" with the figure of the "model'"—a kind of human prop, if you will, a part of the film's plasticity, an automaton that does not "express" himself or herself, but

rather is folded into the film's expressivity: "Models who have become automatic (everything weighed, measured, timed, repeated ten, twenty times) and are then dropped in the medium of the events of your film—their relations with the objects and persons will be *right*, because they will not be *thought*."[3] Although Bresson refers to both objects and persons, his modeling of the person draws the latter close to the object and thus, we would argue, creates an expanded category of what we refer to as the prop.

At another point, Bresson writes: "Actors, costumes, sets and stage furniture are bound to make one think at once of the stage. Take care that the persons and objects in my film may not make people think at once of the cinematographer."[4]

Bresson is perhaps one of the most generous theorists of the cinematic prop, given that most of his imperatives for making genuine film art consist in treating everything in the profilmic with the considered imperiousness and instrumentality one associates with prop management. Bresson points to a truth of the prop: namely, that its falsehood—its ability to represent this or that—will always be the outcome of a process of a yoking of the thing-in-the-world into the service of the story-to-be-told. In this sense, he leads us to consider what might be a radical instrumentality that subtends the practice of filmmaking and the medium of cinema.

We prop ourselves up on Bresson's writing somewhat, as a means of indicating the scarcity of actual thinking on the prop in cinema that names itself as such. The cinematic prop is an under-thought category in film studies (unlike in theater studies). And when the prop is thought, it may often be done so only implicitly, when a theorist refers to an "object" or "thing" captured by the camera. The prop is oddly central to the history of film theory; it undergirds some of the most categorical claims filmmakers and theorists have made about the nature of the medium. But film theory's discourse on the prop is a fugitive discourse. The theorization of the prop has been hidden in plain sight within discourses of the object, on the mute stuff that arrays sets, and the force of the camera's claim and capacity to capture things. We turn to this history of critical thought in order to better understand what Siegfried Kracauer called the "thicket of things."[5] How might what we know about film theory be rearranged and emboldened by seeing the prop as the uncredited buttressing agent for so many of its extraordinary claims?

Props among Things

Some of this terrain has been recently mapped from writers invested in a broader conception of the thing in film theory. Volker Pantenburg, in the edited collection *Cinematographic Objects*, addresses the terrain of discursive affinities between developments in humanistic scholarship around the philosophical question of the object and the rise of "thing theory."[6] Such tendencies are variously emergent in object-oriented ontology, actor-network theory, speculative realism, and new materialism—diverse areas of thought all defined by a return to the thing. Pantenburg positions these developments in relation to an opportunity to see in film practices and histories a possible revival of the question posed by film theorists and critics of the 1920s: that is, "What do films and cinema teach us about objects? By means of what kinds of operations does the medium shift agency to the material, inanimate world?"[7] Although we share a sensibility with such approaches to the question, Pantenburg's collection stretches the question a bit too broadly (for our tastes), and in so doing makes the object a unit and sequence in an equivalential chain of other objects. Objects proliferate and objects multiply across scales. As this move expands the domain of the cinematic object (in films, of films) and of the cinema as object in both directions, what is lost is the specificity and historicity of the "propness of the prop," its biddenness as a particular and peculiar condition of the cinematic experience. By hewing closely to the prop and reading the profuse film theoretical discourses of the twentieth century for the *propness* of its things, we aim to re-center the specific and heretofore invisible labors of the film prop in its constitution of an understanding of cinema. Although the prop may appear a minor player, or a supporting character in the larger work of mise-en-scène, and thus a subordinate "unit" of filmic meaning, we argue that it uniquely discloses a field of relations that attest to cinema's singularity as a medium of capitalist modernity.

The "return to things" so prevalent in recent philosophical discourses cannot circumvent the centrality of Heidegger's thinking on the thing. One of the most famous discursive props in the history of philosophy is an earthenware jug, an example of what Heidegger calls a "thing." Suggestively, perhaps, his essay begins with the "shrinking" of distances, with a familiar narrative of modern alienation in which film makes a starring appearance: "Distant sites of the most ancient cultures are shown on film as if they stood this very moment amidst today's street traffic."[8] Seeing the pyramids in a film from a seat in a movie theater in Philadelphia is an example of "the frantic abolition of distances" that "brings no nearness."[9] Things, for Heidegger, in this essay at least, are one way of occasioning a nearness that is not merely "distanceless" (his term). Thingness is a mode of presencing. The Thing names the agent of this presencing or bodying forth. So when Heidegger says, in a delightful Teutonic tautology that "the thing things" he is being less cryptic than he might immediately sound.[10] He means that the thing enacts this process of bringing the thing into our apprehension, of creating nearness. If the thing things, can we say that the prop props? The prop may not (*pace* Heidegger) "near" the world. It subtends a world that is not the world but is an image, a representation of the world. The prop is the extra of the material world, of the world of things. When functioning properly, the prop might be understood to disappear into itself.

Could, however, the extrusion of the bad prop, the magnified prop, bring us near to a sense of either the gimcrackery of the fictional world, or else the radical alterity and density of the prop as a thing that exists before the camera and continues to exist when the camera turns away? Does weak narrativity bring us closer to the world's things, in other words? The prop is intended to make effective the representation, to conceal artifice, or to congeal an image of the world. Its promise is to secure, to clasp the representation into place; its threat is to shove itself too far into view, to draw too near, to assert, if not its Heideggerian thingness, then its objective, autonomous objecthood.

Magnification and Mobility of the Prop

In a compelling essay that is one of the most extended meditations on props in film studies, Lesley Stern calls the intentional "theatricalization" of a thing's presence before the camera a "histrionic" propensity.[11] Avatars of this propensity include Charlie Chaplin and Buster Keaton, in whose films "the democratization of people and things is a structural axiom generative of performance," as well as Michael Powell and Emeric Pressburger, who afford visions of a world "where things and people are similarly mobile and mimetic."[12] Opposed, or dialectically related to this propensity, is the "quotidian," represented by early actualities, the work of Vittorio De Sica, or by a film like Chantal Akerman's *Jeanne Dielman, 23, quai du Commerce, 1080 Bruxelles* (1975).

The histrionic propensity Stern names as one trajectory of the prop's registry of signs is expressed clearly by Jean Epstein, a writer Stern discusses, and clearly a determinative figure for the discourse of the cinematic thing. In his "On Certain Characteristics of *Photogénie*" from 1924, Epstein writes:

> A close-up of a revolver is no longer a revolver, it is the revolver-character, in other words the impulse toward or remorse for crime, failure, suicide. It is as dark as the temptations of the night, bright as the gleam of gold lusted after, taciturn as passion, squat, brutal, heavy, cold, wary, menacing. It has a temperament, habits, memories, a will, a soul. . . . Mechanically speaking, the lens alone can sometimes succeed in revealing the inner nature of things in this way.[13]

The cinematic thing, given an interiority and latent will of its own by the "mechanical brain" of the camera, signals the tumult of narrative signs, themes, and symbols, an ocean of contradictory feelings. Here, and in other essays, among them, "The Cinema Seen from Etna" (1926), Epstein invokes cinema's "'animism'": "On screen, nature is never inanimate. Objects take on air. Trees gesticulate. Mountains, just like Etna, convey meanings. Every prop becomes a character."[14] While taking account of film theory's relatively early state of development when Epstein was writing, we gently resist the anthropocentric move that inheres in the likening of the prop to a character, another human actor. We feel more comfortable sticking closer to Bresson's likening of the character (model, actor) to a prop, rather than the other way around, for reasons we hope to make clear a bit later.

For Epstein the animacy and animation of the prop, which moves at times into an anthropomorphic equivalence, hinges on a subtle or at times overt mystification that subtends much cinephilic writing of this period, a movement toward the thing's revelationist enchantment. Movement's tremors give vibrancy to staid, stolid, and presumably passive matter, as the transformative motility of cinematic time, the alchemical capacities of celluloid, and the filmstrip's inscription of light and shade grant the object a gesticulating formal expressivity.

In his own films Epstein's fascination with cinematic objects and their capacity to sediment and telescope otherworldly emotions finds its utmost manifestation. In *The Three-Sided Mirror* (1927) props enhance the mercurial mystery of Paul (René Ferté), the film's dashing and cruel protagonist, a dandyish, dispassionate Lothario. Paul is the object of desire and puzzlement of the three women who narrate their relationship to him in a series of flashbacks. Each of these elaborates the nature of Paul's insolence as he abandons woman after woman, preferring his car and the thrill of its speed. In the recollections of Pearl (Olga Day), who recounts his alternately tyrannical and serene demeanor, a scene of the two in an art-deco parlor emphasizes an intersubjective tug of war through the oneiric capacity of props. The camera's fixation on the telephone that sits on Paul's desk is used to emphasize Paul's infatuation with velocity and technicity rather than with any romantic attachment. As Pearl sits, waiting impatiently for his attention, the telephone acts as an inhuman interruptive agent, a third partner of this fraught romance. Amid the mixed signals of attraction and dereliction that pass between Pearl and Paul, the camera tracks into a close-up of the telephone's spherical polished metal receiver and, with its gaze, bestows to the camera a vibratory quality. The scene pictures Pearl's human desire for Paul and Paul's restless desire for mechanized movement. A cutaway shot shows electrical and telephone lines on which birds are perched. A jeweled ring appears from a box, revealed in close-up as seductive distraction. Paul throws it at Pearl to appease her; it lands by her feet near a baroque woven pillow. She tries on the ring, then jumps up to embrace him. They move in to kiss, an act which is interrupted by the ringing of the phone. A close-up of the round polished opening summons their gazes. The camera tracks in to a close-up of the phone's smooth surface, then cuts to a close-up of Pearl's supplicating lips, parting open in entreaty. Epstein presents the telephone as a hypnotic, ominous force, at once threatening, cold, and carnal, one that exerts a magnetic power that (from an unseen space) beckons Paul and the film spectator. Analogous to, yet in excess of the transfixing potency of the fleshy human face seen in close-up, the shot of the telephone radiates with inexplicable animistic energy. The shot exemplifies Christophe Wall-Romana's description of Epstein's practice: his "vision of the singularity of filmic objects, preserving ... the filmed object's gaze-like emanation." Further, Wall-Romana notes that "Epstein's paradigmatically photogenic objects—a telephone, a gun, a door handle—... convey inter-human involvement: they crystallize intersubjectivity into a material form disclosed through the film's singularized motion."[15] In another essay, "For a New Avant-Garde," following a discussion of the rich possibilities offered by the telephone onscreen, Epstein states that "it seems very mysterious to me that one can ... charge the simple reflection of inert objects with an intensified sense of life, that one can animate it with its own vital import." In this passage Epstein makes the case for "cinematic telepathy," which exceeds for him the use of mere aesthetic techniques or "mechanical devices."[16] In cinematic telepathy, the "personality" of the object (the prop!), saturated by memory, feeling, intersubjectivity, and metabolized by cinematic reproducibility embodies, enfolds, and discloses cinema's essence.

In both his writing and films Epstein's manner of thinking the relationship between the prop and the cinema, a tendency he shares with such writers as Germaine Dulac, Louis Delluc, Dziga Vertov, Siegfried Kracauer, and Louis Aragon, has been framed by Pantenburg as an "object-oriented filmology,"[17] one that foregrounds questions of the material world's agency through the specifically cinematic object. Aragon, too, in his essay "On Decor," stages the decisive nature of cinema's things in its power as poetic medium, as he writes in a celebrated passage,

> All our emotion exists for those dear old American adventure films that speak of daily life and manage to raise to a dramatic level a banknote on which our attention is riveted, a table with a revolver on it, a bottle that on occasion becomes a weapon, a handkerchief that reveals a crime, a typewriter that's a horizon of a desk, the terrible unreeling ticker tape with its magic ciphers that enrich or ruin bankers.... On the screen objects that were a few moments ago sticks of furniture or books of cloakroom tickets are transformed to the point where they take on menacing or enigmatic meanings. The theater is powerless where such emotive concentration is concerned.[18]

Aragon's litany of objects finds parallels throughout the work of many other early cinephilic critics who describe the power of things suddenly transformed by cinema. One could think too about how that litany of exemplary objects is itself a figuring of an encounter with cinema's creation of material concepts, an aesthetic scene in which the collection of things is a pretext for thinking the disordered plenum of modernity, encountered as an enchantment with the panoramic variety of stuff from which an autonomous gaze plucks out a specimen for its work.[19] Aragon's characterization of that force emphasizes the transformative capacity of the cinema as revelatory medium, achieved through duration and the potential of enlargement to catalyze the prop's emotional potency.

Grasping at Props: Cinephilia as Possession

For Aragon, the cinema of Chaplin and its utilization of decor—from his cane and hat to the many objects and machines, large and small, that he handles and collides with—is central to the tragic and absurd nature of his comedy; Aragon asserts that "nothing is useless ... and nothing indispensable. The decor is Charlie's very vision of the world which together with the discovery of the mechanics and its laws, haunts the hero to such an extent that by an inversion of values, each inanimate object becomes a living thing for him, each human person a dummy whose starting handle must be found."[20] Aragon suggests that the thresholds created by the collision of humans and things in Chaplin's comedy, and the reorganization of filmic decor ultimately unleash "a thousand social cataclysms."[21] Chaplin's exemplary model for Aragon rests on the postulate that nothing exceeds or escapes use or waste—nothing is "useless" or "indispensable." The central paradox of use in waste and waste in use gets us to the spectral core of the prop's unstable centrality at the heart of the cinematic thing. No prop is ever new; it is always in some sense used and reused, sometimes entirely used up. The constant yoking of the object to use value gets at some of the ways that the *prop* (rather than the thing) hinges on cinema's harnessing of both objects and people in a system of employment.

In her positioning of cinematic things as continuous with and dependent on the operations of gesture, Stern folds what might seem the more discrete category of the prop into an imagining of the material and immaterial propensities of cinematic things to harness movement, to interact with bodies in a choreographic ensemble of habits, tics, graspings, maneuvers. In doing this, the cinematic thing as articulated and extended by Stern tends towards a register of dissolution and evaporation. Homing in on the cigarette as her privileged example, Stern sees in the cinematic thing a facility for movement and a tendency toward evanescence. The cigarette operates as an ur-prop and glorious augmenter of character. Yet in its transformation through burning, through its smoke and particulate dissipation, it permeates boundaries between bodies, spaces, and things, dissolving into atmosphere. Stern configures the cinematic thing into a capricious category, one that appears more conceptually capacious than the prop in the terms of her argument. Her insights rest on an investment in the thing's undecidability and ephemerality, its route to the central ambivalences and ambiguities within film form's hewn materiality. Our examination here reframes the questions Stern poses, moving in the opposite direction. How might the prop's concretion and utility suggest a central problematic within the film medium's drive to make the world its instrument?

Francesco Casetti has recently synthesized Epstein's thinking about objects in the following manner: "Cinema ... allows us to become conscious of the objects that surround us, after we have long since taken them for granted to the point that we are no longer conscious of their existence.... Cinema offers itself as a site of revelation and of encounter: the spectator can once more grasp and interact with the fabric of the world."[22] Here Casetti (as he well knows) is nearly paraphrasing Viktor Shklovsky's famous essay "Art as Device," in which he reminds us that we have been "given the tool of art ... in order to make us feel objects, to make a stone feel stony."[23]

The grasping, grabby, possessive spectator Casetti posits is, however, rather irksome. Epstein's decision to impute personality (if not personhood) to the object onscreen anthropomorphically aligns the object with human consciousness, thus turning the object—the revolver, the prop par excellence perhaps, given its centrality to numerous genres, plot twists and resolutions, etc.—into a prop for human thought. The prop is a medium for another medium. The worn-out human relationship to the world finds cinema to hand as a means of re-enchanting this world, and this re-enchantment proceeds by way of finding to hand the things of the world and radically magnifying, estranging, making them "new"—not in and of themselves, but new to human perception and cognition. This process of transformation and transmutation is also riven with ambivalence.

There is a tendency in classical film theory to cast the conceptual and sensual terrain to which film grants us access as virgin territory. Whatever cinema is, however, we should not see it as a means of granting us unfettered access to an unsullied plenitude. Cinema is predicated on an imaginary of repetition, reproduction, possession, and use—and of possession grounded in use. Its imaginary is subtended by the real enactments of these processes (in the medium's native nineteenth century and before). The prop, fundamental to film's enactment of its own mediatized presence, its narrativization and psychologization of the world and its objects, becomes, as it were, the handle by which we can grab hold of this foundational problematic. By seeing the prop as the means by which cinema and its theorization carry out its magnification of reality, its re-presencing and "redemption" of the world and everyday life, we are able to grasp not cinema's essence or essential aesthetic properties, but cinema's instrumental core.

Our use of the term "redemption" is meant to bring to mind Kracauer's *Theory of Film: The Redemption of Physical Reality*. In chapter 3, "The Establishment of Physical Existence," Kracauer notes that "the hunting ground of the motion picture camera is in principle unlimited; it is the external world expanding in all directions."[24] This is an innocuous enough metaphor at first sight, and yet seeing the encounter between camera and world in terms of capture and (animal) slaughter brings again to our attention how much film theory's imaginary is haunted by quasi-colonialist fantasies of discovering a "new" world. We might recall at this point that the word "redeem" has a complex signification: It can signify spiritual salvation, but it can also mean, in a more material register, the gaining or regaining of possession.

In the same chapter Kracauer writes that "there are certain subjects within ... [the] world that may be termed 'cinematic' because they exert a peculiar attraction on the medium."[25] These subjects include "movement," "inanimate objects," and "things normally unseen." It is in his consideration of "inanimate objects," that Kracauer draws nearest to an explicit discussion of the prop. First glossing Louis Delluc's interest in objects that, when carefully observed by the camera, relegate the actor to being "no more than a detail, a fragment of matter of the world," Kracauer goes on to write that

> the urge to raise hats and chairs to the status of full-fledged actors has never completely atrophied. From the malicious escalators, the unruly Murphy beds, and the mad automobiles in silent comedy to the cruiser Potemkin, the oil derrick in *Louisiana Story* and the dilapidated kitchen in *Umberto D.*, a long procession of unforgettable objects has passed across the screen—objects which stand out as protagonists and all but overshadow the rest of the cast.[26]

About less—to borrow Stern's term—"histrionic" cinematic objects, those that "merely serve as a background to the self-contained dialogue and the closed circuit of human relationships," Kracauer merely says that they are "essentially uncinematic."[27] This is a throwaway passage, to some extent, but one perhaps worth taking seriously. Despite his radical theoretical openness to the undramatic and quotidian,

Kracauer here privileges the cinematic magnification and personification of objects—the stylized manipulation of props—as the means by which cinema demonstrates the possession of its "properties." But the background prop—the chair that is just there—actually comes closer to the interest in ordinariness that is the origin myth in Kracauer's preface, where he recalls a vision of "an ordinary suburban street" glimpsed fleetingly in his first outing to the cinema.

The worrying thing, or the apparently harmless thing that we, at any rate, want to worry about, is how, in order to assert its own individuation as a medium—its "personality," its specificity, its *claim* on uniqueness—the cinema must lay claim to the world and its objects. It must turn the world into its prop, or, in other, less innocuously abbreviated terms, its property.

When we home in more specifically on particular objects (things) appropriated by or made for the cinema, we see that the prop props up a belief in the essential property of cinema: It is the thing around or on which this property accretes. Here we must consider the prop's relationship to the close-up and the close-up's relationship to the prop. The close-up has been understood as one of the signs of the cinema itself, one of the signatures of the medium: a durational moving image of something blown up and projected on-screen far in excess of the size of the object in real life. Mary Ann Doane writes that for a theorist like Epstein, "the close-up is the privileged site" for *photogénie*, Epstein's term, as we know, for what Doane calls "the very essence of cinematic specificity."[28] For Doane, the close-up is almost inevitably linked to the representation of the human face. Although it is true that the close-up is consistently drawn to the face, in fact, there are two other main competitors for the intimacy of the camera's attention: human hands and objects—or props. The close-up is a formal gesture, a convention, a rhetorical figure, an idiom that is both gigantic and miniaturizing. Although its theorization by such writers as Béla Balázs has often, in fact, emphasized its attraction to objects (props), these objects have, when viewed in close-up, been turned into humans, as if that were the magical property bestowed on props: to be like us. But if we resist this cloying anthropomorphism that wants to see the human in everything the camera looks at, then we see that the close-up is allied with, dependent on, interested in things, things that are not humans, things that are props. The prop thus plants itself in the center of cinema's courtship of and enchantment with the human and forces us to tell a different story about it. Because even though we have in these pages made the prop speak, let us insist instead on not simply its muteness, which is still a category bound to speech and articulation, but on its objective alterity, its silence. (Things that should talk but cannot are mute. Things that just don't talk are silent.) The point, however, is that the prop finds itself under the close-up's microscope. Does the prop have an inorganic charisma that rivals that of the human parts that so frequently occupy the close-up? If some theorists of *photogénie* see faces in things (Epstein posits the object's intrinsic "personality"), could we not turn the argument around and see the prop as a contaminating agent that sees *faces* as things? Is the face, in the end, not just a prop for cinema's love affair with its own properties?

A similar movement of thought is found in Bazin's "The Virtues and Limitations of Montage," an essay that might be considered a meditation on the manipulation of the prop in order to produce a sense of the "unity of space."[29] Comparing Albert Lamorisse's *The Red Balloon* (1956) to Jean Tourane's *The Secret of Magic Island* (1957), Bazin argues that the illusion of a red balloon's animated liveliness and its "zoomorphism" requires the limiting of montage devices and the production of an extensible spatiotemporal field. Bazin approaches something like what Bresson seems to mean, when he writes, "If the film is to fulfill itself aesthetically, we need to believe in the reality of what is happening while knowing it to be tricked."[30] The agent (and the medium) of this trickery is the prop.

"Reading for the prop" is what we are proposing here: returning to familiar texts, familiar notions, beliefs about and investments in cinema and the "cinematic" in order to understand what sorts of appropriations subtend the articulations of film's claim to propertied-ness. Another way of saying this might be that thinking about the prop is a way of desublimating our understanding of cinema as a revelatory medium in order to see it (simultaneously) as an appropriative medium. Film is a medium that is founded on a kind of primitive accumulation of the earth's resources, one whose theorization is made possible by the ascription to it of essential properties that are made visible by the instrumental appropriation of property itself.

The other thing that this focus on the prop can produce is an awareness of the prop's relationship to labor. In Shklovsky's famous passage about art's ability to reveal to us the stoniness of the stone, he closes with a comment in italics: "*Art is a means of experiencing the process of creativity. The artefact itself is quite unimportant.*"[31] All of the attempts to bring the prop into close view—to bring it into nearness—are also attempts, via the cinematic medium, to bring into nearness the world itself; all of these depend on "the process of creativity," a dialectical struggle of the human with materials, things, and technology. Whether vividly presented to us by the extravagance of the close-up (witness: labor of the cinematographer) or discreetly disclosed to us in its matter-of-fact existence in the background of some domestic mise-en-scène (witness: labor of the set designer, the art department, the property department, the research department, etc.), the prop explicitly and implicitly drags labor into view. The prop props, yes, and the prop props open a door through which we see not just the magic of the world, but the way in which labor exerts itself, appropriates the world's surfaces as property through which cinema's properties can be assembled.

Part of what we are driving at is merely an illumination of a razor-thin distinction between an ideological critique of the medium itself and an account of the way in which film gives us pleasure. This is an account of the appropriation and subsequent deployment and enjoyment of the spoils that make film possible. The prop holds out the reminder that what we look for at and in the cinema is predicated, however unconsciously, on a possessive, extractive attitude to the world. If we are lucky, we will find this encounter with the medium and its props to be bracing and discomfiting. Contending with the prop may not exactly offer us the means by which we eventually overcome our love affair with possession, which is the sign of our real dispossession and alienation. But the prop might be a place, as good as any, from which to start.

3

Prop Value

Vincente Minnelli's *The Bad and the Beautiful* (1952) is a two-hour hymn to the prop. In it we witness what might be an apotheosis of the prop as the ontological substance of the Hollywood mode of production. As a film that began its life as a literary "property" about a tyrannical theater director before being translated into a meta-cinematic spectacle of high Hollywood irony, *The Bad and the Beautiful* forces us to share a double vision of the props that overcrowd its scenes. Its debt to Orson Welles's *Citizen Kane* (1941—more on which in the following chapter) is brandished ostentatiously: We have Kirk Douglas as Jonathan Shields, a Welles- and Kane-like megalomaniacal film producer-cum-director who both destroys the lives and vivifies the careers of director Fred (played by Barry Sullivan), starlet Georgia Lorrison (Lana Turner), and a novelist-screenwriter James Lee Bartlow (Dick Powell). The homage to *Kane* is further elaborated by these three acting successively as a trio of intradiegetic voice-over narrators. But perhaps the richest vein of relation to Welles's film is the magnificent scale of the mise-en-scène. As we watch the events unfold, we are implicitly compelled to

tabulate the inventory of MGM's property department, much of which seems to have been put on display before us.

About midway through the film, we see Jonathan and Georgia celebrate her growing comfort in the movie they are shooting. Jonathan opens a demi of champagne; we watch his facility with the cork, the ease with which he pours out two coupes and toasts Georgia on her advancing career. (Champagne bottles and glasses have a prolific career as props in cinema.) This calculatedly carefree bit of "business" occupies the foreground of the shot just as, in the background, the door to Jonathan's office is thrown open and in walk three members of the production team, one of them—the only woman in the group—awkwardly transporting an architectural model of one of the film's sets in her arms. In other words: in the foreground, the deft manipulation of props (whose reality is exhibited by the actual popping of the cork and the actual ingestion of the champagne) by a skilled actor portraying a deft manipulator of the people around him, including his starlet lover, whose own accelerating ability to act and perform is exactly what occasions this toast; and in the background, the (intentionally) awkward handling of a prop by an actor portraying a stereotyped supporting character (the bumbling assistant). This latter prop is a model of something that does not exist, something presented to us to signify the excessive and labor-intensive mode of production of the fictional film-within-the-film. We might think initially that the champagne coupes and the champagne itself are the props that prick us most with the sense of their reality: their physical presence—the nonfictional usefulness of the glasses and the nonfictional potability of the fizzy liquid (it might actually be champagne!) that they carry to Lana Turner's and Kirk Douglas's lips. Meanwhile, the prop that is the architectural model is obviously something that we would rightly assume was fabricated by the MGM art department merely for the purposes of the representation of this fictional world, and thus has less purchase on the material real. And yet this model, *because* we know or assume it has no life outside the production of *The Bad and the Beautiful*, ushers into view the unsung collaborative labors of the art and property departments. Figure and ground, foreground and background are occupied by people, but these people are preoccupied by props. The props fasten and focus our attention on what could be the ineffable activity of acting itself or the generic working out of a plot that brazenly advertises its foregone conclusions from the film's first moments.

The mise-en-abîme structure of *The Bad and the Beautiful* is intricately entwined with its prop work. As with *Sunset Boulevard* (Billy Wilder, 1950), *Singing in the Rain* (Stanley Donen and Gene Kelly, 1952), or *The Player* (Robert Altman, 1992), the film's reflexivity is its denoted content, not a secret or something to be decoded. The props that we see in this film, in their vintage Minnelli-esque overabundance and stylized disposition before the camera, present us with a strangely stubborn kernel of reality against which our watching tests itself. As in any film, a prop is a prop: It goes into, services, enables, subtends the fiction. The gimcrack artisanality of a studio's production of make-believe is as materially real as the *really* real champagne bottle and glasses. Both are there, onscreen, touched by actors' hands and bodies. The prop, as a category, then, might be said to dissolve or gently erode the boundary that should separate the real from the fictional. The prop is not a sovereign agent.[1] How could it be when it never has any say over where it gets set down or who gets to pick it up? It is, however, a solvent that thins the membrane between the real thing and the fictional thing by its insistent monstration of the fact that all things before the camera (and projected onscreen) are things before and for the camera and therefore are, in some irreducible sense, real.[2] In other words, in the set's artificial ecology, the prop serves the needs of fictionality but threatens always to undermine fiction with the force of its own tangible reality.

In a subsequent scene Georgia returns from a period of relaxation in Palm Springs after weeks of rehearsal in the Pygmalion-like grasp of Jonathan's creative will. Jonathan has doggedly coaxed and goaded Georgia's potential (another property) into existence. She appears on the production's empty sound stage on the night before the start of shooting. Her jitters are obvious. The scene reveals the momentarily immobilized set, hushed before the manic production will be put in motion. Wandering amid the chairs of the crew, Georgia enters her dressing room trailer to find a wrapped gift. The gift is from Jonathan, a pearl necklace with a note expressing pride in his budding star's ascension (under his effortful guidance). The gift, yet another transactional acquisition, joins Georgia's creative expressivity to her romantic attachment to Jonathan. Reflexively, this gift, this prop, never casts off the odor of exchange value. Georgia's performance has been secured through Jonathan, through his romantic belief in her potential, which he has mined as yet another resource to be extracted, refined, and used up. This gift, in its surplus status, whether given earnestly or cynically, sends Georgia careening into an alcoholic spiral of self-sabotage. She abandons the production by pulling a no-show the next morning. The shaping of human labor is depicted through an economy of gifts that signals the unpayable debt as well as the failure of recompense. If the pearl necklace interrogates the film's ironic view of creative labor and the exploitation that undergirds it, it also lingers as an image of investment—of Jonathan's investment of capital and emotional energy in the fantasy of Georgia's ascension as ingenue, and in a romantic cathexis that is apparently required in order to generate the immaterial labor of acting. The necklace as prop reveals an economistic logic of acquisition and expenditure, of gathering and using up, even as it gestures to a rubric of love, which is, nonetheless, exposed as yet another illusion necessary for the production of yet another illusion.

The property department's existence as standing reserve for the needs of spectacular narrativization is explicitly acknowledged in *The Bad and the Beautiful* in a scene in which a visitor to the studio, Rosemary (Gloria Grahame)—the wife of James Lee Bartlow, the Southern writer who has been recruited to adapt the script of Jonathan's new production—marvels at the wonders it holds. This is a slightly unnecessary, even tautological scene, with regard to the plot's advancement: It makes little happen. It occasions a glimpse of the softening of James Lee's resistance to Jonathan's overtures, but at its close, his joining the production is still left in doubt. The dialogue further sketches in Rosemary's character as a silly, easily impressed and distracted Southern belle, whose inconsequential and incontinent conversation threatens to interrupt, delay, or derail her husband's creative labors. This trait of Rosemary's, however, has already been firmly established in prior scenes that lead up to this tour of the studio. The scene is, in other words, excessive insofar as it is largely superfluous to the needs of the plot. It simultaneously presents us with the excessive nature of studio production in general—its inordinate consumption of resources, labor—and of this picture (the film within the film) in particular. It begins with a dense medium shot in which we are shown Rosemary in the foreground, James Lee just behind her, and Jonathan and other members of his production team visible in the further background. But everywhere around these living human figures crowd the dead objects of the property warehouse. Rosemary's attention seems to be caught by what looks like an eighteenth-century porcelain miniature of a man kneeling before a woman in an attitude of courtship, while at her back a life-size bronze of a helmeted warrior figure (or possibly the god Hermes?) menaces her with a raised fist. To her left, an overstuffed Victorian armchair, next to it a chandelier wrought of metal and crystal in a floral design, and all around, above and below, in the extreme fore- and background are what seem to be hundreds of other useful and ornamental items, all waiting in store. The camera pans and dollies, keeping a thoroughly enthralled Rosemary in the center of the frame, but revealing, again, more and more props: statues, braziers, vases, endless shelves jammed with bric-a-brac, the vast majority of which can barely be discerned in any distinctness, but whose numerousness creates an image of sheer abundance. Each prop—especially the smaller ones that we cannot clearly make out in the background—and all of the props taken as a congregated whole constitute an image of the magnificent scale of the Hollywood mode of production.

How can we understand Rosemary's interest in the inestimable value of the props she regards with such amazement? She is stopped in her tracks by an enormous Queen Anne dining room table set for twelve, with a large crystal chandelier hovering just above. Rosemary exclaims in delighted astonishment *and* recognition: "Why, look here, James Lee, the dining room at Rowan Oak, just the way we saw it when you wrote it." "Just the way I saw it when I read it," Jonathan replies. "Look at that chandelier! Why it's Waterford, isn't it?" "Yes, Mrs. Bartlow, it is," replies a member of the production team. A few moments later, Rosemary interrupts Jonathan's professional courtship of James Lee by announcing, "There's never been such silver, not even in Richmond." A few more lines of dialogue are exchanged between James Lee and Jonathan, and the scene ends with the visiting Southern couple being put in a taxi and driven away, as Jonathan, laughing at Rosemary's chatty intrusiveness, remarks, "No wonder it took him seven years to write a book." The derisory attitude toward Rosemary proleptically gestures towards the plot's eventual disposal of her. Seeing that, in fact, her garrulous company is an obstacle to James Lee's production of his screenplay, Jonathan sends her away with one of his actors, only for both to end up dying in a plane crash. Rosemary's ephemerality and disposability here seem to be weighed against the durability of the props that so enthralled her. The prop might be more durable, it seems, than those who handle it.

More difficult to parse than the contest between the obduracy of the prop and the impermanence of human flesh, however, is the nature of Rosemary's interest in these props. She is struck by their reality: They are no different than the things they will represent on-screen. In fact, they *are* the things they will represent on-screen. And they are valuable. Waterford crystal and silver better than one can find in the state of Virginia: These movie props are identical to and indistinguishable from their counterparts in the world—in auction houses, or in the grand houses of Southern ladies like Rosemary herself. These props exceed the value of the silver place settings one might find in Richmond. Perhaps the film industry can afford objects of greater rarefaction than the scions of Virginia's first families. Or perhaps what strikes Rosemary as their extraordinary value consists in the fact these props are real *and* will become fictionalized, once they have been incorporated into the film. But Rosemary's delight is misplaced and explains part of the reason why she exists to be gotten rid of: Her over-invested stupefaction at the prop-as-commodity's extraordinary value might get in the way of the prop's mere use value. The prop's value consists in its endless fungibility, its availability, over and over, for use.

Early commentators on the US motion picture industry in the period of its budding maturity in the 1920s were attuned to the complex nature of the prop's value. In 1922, film publicist Melvin M. Riddle, in a light-hearted sketch of the various departments of the film studio and their attendant contributions to the production process, writes that "properties might be said to have two values, one computed from a cold, commercial standpoint, the other contingent upon the usefulness of the articles to the studio, and the amount of labor and time that was spent in securing them."[3] All of which is to say that the prop is always (or quite often) just another commodity, one whose value is not strictly determined by its use but by the social relations that are encrypted in the commodity as an item of exchange value. Rosemary's enchantment with Waterford chandeliers and the superior silver flatware in the property department's warehouse is right, after all: The prop is but one more example of Marx's understanding of the commodity as a "social hieroglyphic."[4] The prop's putative value—for the film and in the film's diegesis—is returned to obsessively, indeed, is thematized at key moments in the narrative of *The Bad and the Beautiful*. This foregrounding of the prop brings into view some of the ways in which the prop operates in a manner that might be grasped by Marx's critique of political economy.

We are now prepared to introduce a term that we will call "prop value." The lexicon of Marxist analysis leads us here, in part because it is so clearly germane to our attempts to apprehend the prop's function. In its seductive proximity to the commodity, the prop teases and tests the explanatory value of Marxist analysis. The prop cannot be understood without reference to Marx, but the terms of Marxist analysis meet a limit in the prop's tendency simultaneously to assimilate and resist them.

The value of the prop, when integrated into filmmaking practice, becomes part of the film's exchange value. Such an augmentation of value can be seen clearly when a prop is purchased by the property department, stored and reused again and again in production after production. This sort of prop and the uses made of it constitute an example of what Marx calls "constant capital": those "instruments of labor" that, unlike human labor, are not entirely used up and extinguished in the labor process.[5] The prop may eventually need to be replaced—should a champagne coupe be dropped by an actor, for instance—but the expenditure occasioned by its initial purchase will have been more than worth the original investment in terms of the surplus value extracted from it each time it is pulled out of the prop warehouse and placed on set before the camera's consuming eye. It is in the nature of the prop to exist as a site and a means of value extraction and production. We might say it lends itself to the film, but there is nothing free here; it is merely subject to the intentions of the property master who oversees its deployment and redeployment in the forcing house that is the film set. It might be useful to recall that "to work" does not only denote the (free or enforced) contribution of one's labor; "to work" also means to function, to perform according to the designs of the laborer who manipulates the instrument, or prop. Thus Bill McLaughlin, the studio property master at Burbank Studios in 1986, can say of his props, in a way that initially startles us but finally makes perfect sense: "These are all props. You can't think of them as antiques. Everything in here works."⁶ The prop always sits in the shadow cast by the labor process. And thus, in this relative obscurity, its value consists not in its estimated price on the auction market, but in its durable availability for use.

The prop is obviously, of course, and in several senses, a commodity. For one, it may actually have simply been purchased by the property department. Chandeliers, a plastic toothbrush, or a child's doll: Such props might be procured at a department store and inserted into the film production. In these instances we might think of the prop as being "real," insofar as it exists independently of the film production process. (A "real prop," however, tests our appetite for the oxymoronic when trying to parse the prop's artificial reality and real artifice.) In those instances in which the prop is produced expressly for the film, with no other life for it foreseen beyond the production—what we might think of as a "fake" prop—the prop's status as commodity is less certain. It is a product of human labor (labor-power itself being the ultimate commodity, or the first commodity) and, as we have already mentioned, it is used as an instrument of labor that is useful in producing the strange commodity that is the finished film. Is it like thread or woven linen fabric (examples of the commodity form favored by Marx)? Or is it like the spindle or loom on which the fabric is woven (again, commodities that are also examples of constant capital)? The prop participates in—or rather performs—the fluctuating and virtuosically multiple and multiplying lives of the commodity and the commodity's variable existence as the *means toward* and *product of* the labor process. In this sense it is like every other commodity.

If we are going to entertain the prop's relationship to the commodity, we are therefore and perforce entertaining the question of its value. In Marx's language, a commodity, first and foremost, "satisfies human needs."[7] The "use value," in Marx's terms, of a commodity inheres in its utility, its capacity to perform a function, and all commodities are useful in some way. Marx, however, is not interested in the usefulness of commodities, but rather in what it is they all share (whether the commodity in question is iron or corn or a wooden table). They are products of human labor: "Human labour power has been expended to produce them; human labour is accumulated in them."[8] Seeing them thus—seeing them as "crystals" of labor, "the social substance, which is common to them all"—Marx invites us to see them as embodiments not so much of this or that person's individual labor (which he calls concrete labor) but of "human labour in the abstract."[9] As instances of abstract labor, then, we finally understand them as embodiments of *value*—that thing or substance that all commodities have in common, regardless of what they are made of or who made them. Value is what every commodity has in common with every other commodity; it is the common substance that, indeed, makes them commodities that can be exchanged. (The abstraction of exchange value is something specific to capitalism.) The thought or the conviction that any commodity is "worth" anything is a thought about value. Thus, a commodity is always and foremost, despite its material concreteness or seeming particularity, a *medium* for understanding the nature of value itself. Value, in Michael Heinrich's reading of Marx, "isn't a thing like a bread roll, but rather a social relationship that *appears as a tangible characteristic* of a thing."[10]

What happens when we think of the prop in its inevitable proximity to (and at times, identity with) the commodity and therefore consider it as something that embodies value and assists in the production of new values? Would prop value be distinct from use value or exchange value? It is clear that the prop is useful and satisfies a need. Primarily it is useful in creating the conditions for the production of fictionality, narrative, illusion, representation. We won't belabor the obvious here: If you need to represent a conversation around a dinner table, you are going to need a dinner table. Call the property department. Props have use value; this point is easily understood. What about exchange value? A prop might be purchased from an exchange economy: The exchange value of a table bought at a furniture store and installed on a film set, for instance, will have been expressed in the money that changed hands to purchase it. And presumably it might be sold again once it has served its purpose in the mounting and making of the film.

Does any of the above help us in understanding Rosemary's ejaculation, "There's never been such silver, not even in Richmond"? What is she expressing in this unguarded exclamation? Is she speaking the language of prop value? The props that excite Rosemary are real objects of utility that are also props because they are placed in the service of film production. They have a real life, one that has been indefinitely suspended, and they have a second life—a second career, we might say—as things that make representation appear: Their tangibility as objects makes appearance itself apparently tangible. Perhaps it would be better to distinguish more explicitly between two principal modalities of propness. First, there is the "real" prop: The prop whose existence itself is not necessitated by the film's production and which may have been sourced in the (real) world, and whose identity and utility is the same as any other iteration of itself to be encountered in ordinary life. (Local example: the cutlery that enchants Rosemary. Note: We cannot ascertain, based on the visual evidence presented by the film if it is actually silver, or if it surpasses that to be found in Richmond! But the cutlery was without doubt purchased for the production and not fabricated by the art department.) Second, we have the "fake" prop: The prop whose existence is occasioned by the film, produced by the art department, and often used up by the film and quite possibly discarded at the end of the latter's production process. (Local example: the architectural model described above.)

The fascination extorted by the real prop seems twofold: (1) It is actually the same as the thing it represents in real life—that is to say, it is not fake at all; but (2) it will be inserted into the artificiality of the film. This insertion makes the film—something that, like any representation, is in some fundamental sense, fake—real despite its unreality. The fascination of a fake prop is somewhat different. We might consider the number of times collectors have attempted to own the "real" Maltese Falcon, made famous by the eponymous John Huston film of 1941.[11] This film's convoluted plot repeatedly turns on the whereabouts and authenticity of a sixteenth-century jewel-encrusted golden falcon. According to Vivian Sobchack, in her essay on the afterlives of the props used in making the film, "nine or ten" plaster of paris statuettes representing the falcon were fabricated for the film's production.[12] Sobchack tells a story that is as complicated as the plot of the film itself. Asked by a collector to verify the authenticity of the prop, initially a seemingly straightforward request, she encounters a hall of mirrors of relatively worthless "fake" versions of the falcon that were used to promote *The Black Bird* (David Giler, 1975), a parody of *The Maltese Falcon*, as well as an inestimably valuable "copy" of the bird, cast in solid gold in a mould made from one of the original props. In 2013 a version of the falcon believed to be one of the props used in the making of the film sold at auction for $4.1 million. Doubt still continues to hover over the question of the authenticity of this piece of fakery.[13] A nearly worthless object used in the production of a fiction is—by virtue of an overinvestment in the fictional world it furnished—converted into something of inestimable cost. In this manner, the tortured history of the many Maltese falcons in various collectors' hands only confirms Marx's argument about the autonomy of use value and exchange value.

If the fake prop is doing its job in the film (at least in the context of realist representation), then we are not even thinking of it as a prop at all. But later, if we encounter it in the world, this mostly useless object will have value only because we recognize it as having been woven into the film's fictional world. Prop value can thus express two different but related experiences: one, an amazement that what is real can be subsumed into what is unreal; and another, wonder at the possibility of encountering in the three-dimensional fullness of the world what had first been only seen in the two-dimensional phoniness of the film. A corollary of either experience might be that the (real or fake) prop has been used, handled, touched and held by a beloved performer: the ruby slippers worn by Judy Garland in *The Wizard of Oz* (Victor Fleming, 1939) or the Ouija board used by Linda Blair in *The*

Exorcist (William Friedkin, 1973).[14] And so on. In both cases, the prop's having been in—indeed, having constituted—the film endows it with a value that leaves political economy and enters into the sphere of religion. The prop, because having been in X film or having been fondled by Y actor, assumes the status of the relic. It is somehow holy, no longer exactly a part of the world, because it was once a part of the film. Here, prop value nearly steps out of the categories of use and exchange value and hurls itself onto the altar of fascinated stupefaction where it confounds the ordinary circuits of valorization. Of course, and in turn, a prop might also compel the interested collector to wrest it back from the sphere of veneration and attempt to sell it at a high price that it and it only can fetch, as in the example of the bullwhip used by Harrison Ford in the *Indiana Jones* trilogy.[15]

Like the mercantile trade in actual religious relics, the prop is a signal booster for ideology, which, in the case of the prop, is the ideology of capitalist production. But the prop is also a category of perversion. In fact, we might have made all of this simpler by starting with the category of the fetish. To pay or attract attention to an individual prop, or to extract a prop from the film into whose representational fabric it was originally woven, is a perverse activity. In Freud's account, the fetish is a material object (or else an abstracted part of the human body) that sits in some (physical or perceptual) proximity to the genitals and, in a sense, stands in for them in a way that helps the subject, the fetishist, achieve sexual satisfaction, which would otherwise be impossible. The fetish, in a sense, invests a scene of what would otherwise be "normal" sexual satisfaction with an element of fictionality, of dress-up or make-believe. At the same time, for the fetishist, only the fetish (and nothing but the fetish) can satisfy the need at hand: fur, not silk; feet, not hands. While the fetish may have been arrived at unconsciously and by chance, once the fetishist is in its grip, then only that fetish and that fetish alone can suffice. The prop is probably a more flexible category, at least from the perspective of film production: where one prop might do, so might another, and another. And yet, here too, exceptions abound. For example: What compels a filmmaker like Joanna Hogg to populate her semi-autobiographical films (chiefly we might call to mind *The Souvenir,* Parts I and II [2019 and 2021]) with her own possessions and to encourage her actors to use their own personal belongings as props? Can only these props do the work required to conjugate the premise of the film's fictionality? Or does the specter of autobiography demand the actual object (the real prop, not the fake one) and no other?

An anticipation of our thinking here is Kracauer's charming essay titled "Calico-World" (originally written as a radio broadcast in 1926). Kracauer surveys the storehouse of objects that make up Babelsberg, the enormous film studio in the suburbs of Berlin where some of the most iconic films of the Weimar period were shot. Assessing the great repository of odds and ends and fragmented, fragmentary objects that are manufactured and summoned to be set before the camera, Kracauer suggests that for the world to appear on film it must first be broken down, "cut into pieces." The "world is like a child's toy put in a cardboard box," a warehoused assemblage of the scraps that constitute cinematic reality.[16] Kracauer's essay presents the problem of cinematic representation as a problem of the prop. He directs our attention to the entire panorama of the real artificiality that characterizes the film studio. In reference to the "exotic fauna" that populate the grounds of the studio, alongside its many actors and technicians, Kracauer writes: "The baby crocodile is a prop that one can hold in one's hands, but even the fully grown monstrosities are not as dangerous as their lifeless counterparts, which the monkeys fear."[17] The prop begs the question of what is real and what is fake, because the fakery of the studio—and of industrial film production, in general—is all too real. (Ask the monkeys!) The mode of production makes cramped neighbors of copies and originals. The effect is not so much the mistaking of the former for the latter. Rather, the studio presents the problem of confronting the material thereness of what one knows to be fake living its (usually—save the baby crocodiles) inorganic life alongside things that just are what they are: "The old and the new, copies and originals, are piled up in a disorganized heap like bones in catacombs. Only the property man knows where everything is."[18] The primacy granted this worker—the property manager—signals the primacy of the prop itself.

For Kracauer, cinema's specificity is usually understood in its relationship to contingency. Cinema's ability to record the contingent—the fleeting and fortuitous—underwrites his *Theory of Film*. Cinema is open to the world and thus reproduces the world's openness—its possibility to be other than what it seems at any given time. But the word in German for the (film) prop is *requisit*: something indispensable *for* and demanded *by* the film—something it cannot do without. The prop is a necessary element for the elaboration of the contingency of the world. The story to be told in a film—the diegetic world and the events to be represented—is like a viscous bath that congeals around whatever is baptized in it and fixes it in an attitude of necessity. And yet, the materiality of the props that litter and patiently loiter around the studio (waiting to be used again) also demonstrate that they are as much products of will, choice, or caprice as necessity. The prop's oscillation between need and freedom seems to mirror or mimic its indecisive movement between the fake and the real.

The prop, for Kracauer, is the ontological substrate of the cinema as mode of production and as medium of representation. Kracauer articulates the demands cinema imposes on the world's objects, as well as its compulsive consumption and stockpiling of the stuff of modernity. Every object placed before the camera is prop-like in nature—by virtue of its vulnerability to being made useful. This constructed sense of authenticity and the haphazardness of the assembly of warehoused parts that make up a film's world is something that compels Kracauer's wonder as well as his ambivalence regarding the simulacral plenum of cinematic modernity. His interest here is in cinema's "regime of arbitrariness," which "does not limit itself to the world as it is," but moves and invents, makes malleable and plastic the objects within it, mingling "make-believe" objects and real ones, in the service of a fiction's necessities.[19] Whether we are considering a fake composited street lamp, a cathedral, a rampart of a moat, a gathering of live frogs to enliven a bucolic landscape (some of the examples given by Kracauer), all are subject to a logic of fulgent appearance and subsequent obscurity. Once used, virtually all are swept into the non-time of the inventoried prop storehouse, a mausoleum for the products and implements of exhausted labors. Thus the cinema's props "cannot deteriorate into a ruin, because ruins have to be made to order. Here all objects are only what they are supposed to represent at the moment: they know no development over time."[20] The peculiar temporality of the prop for Kracauer is bound to its narrow window of laboring. The prop's punch card onscreen presence determines its non-historicity; it clocks in and clocks out, but remains barred from the gravity of real historical age.

Nature itself can be replicated, mocked up and put to work in the labor of cinematic representation. Kracauer riffs on the production of "natural" light itself in the painting of unnatural suns in the studio: "Nature's suns likewise leave much to be desired. Since they do not function nearly as reliably as floodlights; they are simply locked out of the newest American film studios. Let them go on strike if they want to."[21] Kracauer's unserious suggestion that the sun might withdraw its labor, as if it were just another disaffected employee on the studio payroll, belies his more serious effort to draw our attention to the medium's instrumentalizing capacity to flatten the world, to parcel everything into exchangeable units of value.

Prop value—if indeed this is in any way a coherent and stable term—names a mode of perverse redirection in which the elements of a film's reality and its fictionality become sites for a dispersal and remapping of spectatorial intensities, for the production of new pleasures or the intensification of old ones. The prop cannot outrun the category of value itself. And as a category of art, the prop cannot escape Theodor

Adorno's (somewhat gnomic) dictum that the artwork is the "absolute commodity."[22] As the bit of reality required for the production of unreality and the element of unreality necessary for the staging of reality, the prop dances manically in and around the categories of value that are made visible and mediated by the commodity itself.

4

Realism, or the Prop's Thereness

Does theater studies' understanding of the theatrical prop exhaust or make redundant our inquiry into the nature of the cinematic prop? A question we have been asked: "What's the difference?" Our answer: mediation. Theater takes, and the cinema takes. Cinema takes objects from the world and films them. In being filmed, they become props. Theater takes objects from the world and puts them on stage. In being placed there, they become props. But in placing the object on stage, the theater places it before us, gives it back to us. If we had to, we could run up and grab it. In placing the object before the camera and filming it, and then projecting the image of that thing on the screen before us, cinema tells us that we cannot have the prop: It is property, somebody else's, that is, the film's. We cannot touch it. The property lines around the cinematic prop are more secure than those in the theater. Given that we write here in a tone that is indebted to the work of Stanley Cavell, we might as well quote him: "A

screen is a barrier."[1] And so is a prop. In cinema, a prop is a barrier that sits behind a barrier.

In what is probably the most sustained meditation on the theatrical prop, Andrew Sofer writes that "'all that is on stage is a sign."[2] But the semiosis of the prop-sign is divided between the ipseity of its material presence and its existence as a "nexus of competing ideological codes."[3] Sofer's attention to the prop's onstage presence leads him into strangely enchanted terrain. Writing against the grain of materialist scholars who have emphasized the prop as a site of ideological struggle, Sofer cautions that "we risk losing sight of . . . the sheer *charm* of stage objects. . . . We must remind ourselves that audiences *pay for* [our italics] theatrical spectacle not because they wish to be interpellated, demystified, or decentered, but because they enjoy being entertained, titillated, and (occasionally) disturbed."[4] We do not doubt the prop's fundamental productivity in generating spectacle, whether on the stage or the screen. Nor do we doubt the fetishistic appetites of audiences. At the end of the day, we are all paying for the prop. As theorists of the cinema, we will only say this: While we admit to the prop's alluring charm, we profit from cinema's structuring irony in which the prop is set before us on-screen and therefore remains beyond our reach, something we can never really have.

Unlike the theater, the cinema is a mode of not having the things and bodies before us, of not even seeing them. Christian Metz is eloquent on this subject. The difference of the theater, the opera, and other modes of live spectacle from the cinema consists in the fact that the former "do not consist of *images*, the perceptions they offer to the eye and the ear are inscribed in a true space (not a photographed one), the same one as that occupied by the public during the performance; everything the audience hear and see is actively produced in their presence, by human beings or props which are themselves present."[5] In the cinema, nothing is there: "The actor, the décor, the words one hears are all absent."[6] Regardless of the play in which she performs, if I go to the theater to see Sarah Bernhardt, Metz writes, "I should see Sarah Bernhardt"; at the cinema, "it would be her shadow."[7] To press home his point, Metz supports his argument with reference to the prop: "What is true of Sarah Bernhardt is just as true of an object, a prop, a chair for example." In the theater, the chair can be many things, take on many functions, "but when all is said and done it is a chair." But in the cinema, this chair "will not be there when the spectators see it."[8]

Metz is concerned to identify for us cinema's parsimony-in-abundance. The "unique position of the cinema lies in" its "dual character," possessing "unaccustomed perceptual wealth" while also being "stamped with unreality to an unusual degree."[9] Our surrender to the cinematic signifier happens in part through the sensual immediacy of cinema—the way we are thrown into contact with changing scenes via changing scales of perception, cities seen as anthills, a face seen as a landscape. All is there for us, before us; and yet nothing is. Metz's preoccupation with the uniqueness of the cinema as a medium that is perceptually both rich and impoverished offers a vantage point for understanding the charm of the theatrical prop's presence in distinction from the penurious absence of cinema's world of things. Marking the difference is only a way of throwing open the door on what might be at stake—for us, for the prop. The prop's incidental appearance in Metz's account of the distinction between what is there in the theater and what is not there (but appears so generously to be so) in the cinema is congruent with its more general imbrication in a story about instrumentality, use, and possession. The prop in the theater is right there. Were we unruly spectators, we could but rush the stage, startle the actors, make it—however fleetingly—ours, until security has wrestled us to the ground. We would have failed in the end, but triumphed in the shorter term in our attempt to hold in our hands the tiny material unit of artistic signification that is the prop. We would have won art for life. In the cinema, we have no such luck. Even Uncle Josh believed he might win for one moment before he crashed into the papery two dimensions of the screen. We have not even the luxury of his naïveté. We have only our fluctuating disavowal: That looks real / too bad it does not exist. In the end, absence wins every time; there is nothing to touch, but we must sit for ninety, one hundred, one hundred and twenty minutes of a film's duration watching one person after another (actors, we call them—a race of phonies) fondle and finger the things we see on-screen but cannot ever touch. The prop gets used—by the actors, by the machinations of narrative, by the camera—by being shown to us while always simultaneously being put away, put beyond our reach. In this sense, the prop is put to a second use: It is an instrument with which we are told, endlessly, "Look, but do not touch. Regard? Yes. Possess? Never!"

These reflections inevitably turn us to a central question: Does the prop have a privileged relationship to realism? By realism, we might first intend the fine-grained, illusionistic, fully rounded textual representation of reality (the world) that wants to convince its reader of its fidelity to what is being represented. Realism as the mirror held up to nature, realism as the window onto the world—verisimilitude, in other words. There are many things in the world, and so if a film is going to represent them, then it needs to produce something like an image of this plenitude, or at the very least a cunning cross-section of it, of the real's infinite fecundity.

To go to an obvious place to pin down this problem with some specificity, consider Orson Welles's *Citizen Kane* (1941). At the center of this film is Charles Kane, a monomaniacal collector who leaves behind him a staggering hoard of possessions: artworks, furniture, statuary, houses, bric-a-brac on a monumental scale. The film's final movement shows us this senseless amassing of things. To exhibit this sublime accumulation, Welles must mount an image of things, and the things that stand in for—that represent—these things are things. The accumulation stands in for the accumulation, in chiastic propriety. Of course, some of this is fudged. We see a superfluity of wooden shipping crates, for instance, that we would probably be correct in thinking are empty. So there are in all likelihood fewer things in this shot of things than the shot wants us to believe, in the way that we would be correct in assuming that Dick Hogan (the actor who plays the murdered David in *Rope*) did not spend the duration of the film closed up inside the chest. But even so, there are still a lot of crates on view. The realist, believable image of abundance is constituted by abundance itself: the abundance of props.[10] In this final sequence of *Citizen Kane*, in what is perhaps the most overdetermined example of prop-ness in film history, an impressive crane shot gropes across the assembled vases, urns, phonographs, headboards, globes, and other things to land finally on a small child's sled, just sitting there amid all that stuff. Amazingly, the camera alights on it *just* at the moment a workman collects it in an offhand manner. In the following shot, we see it chucked into a consuming furnace. Conveniently for us and for the camera, it lands just so, right-side up, so that we can see, as the camera nosily dollies in, a word painted on its surface: "Rosebud," the shibboleth that famously catalyzes the entire film's narrative progression, the mystery at the heart of the mystery, a childhood toy, one glimpsed, in an earlier moment in the film. This solution that solves nothing is a bit of matter that is nothing more than a prop. The prop, we see, sits at the heart of the heart of film history, and at the heart of the heart of this history's love affair with and addiction to realism.

Another word that hovers over the evocation of this scene in *Citizen Kane* is contingency, the appearance of which is the guarantor of realism. This significant image is an image of insignificance—an image of wealth, but of wealth embodied in a spectacle of haphazard hoarding in which there is no way of knowing what is important and what is not, what should be incinerated and what should be preserved. In his essay "The Reality Effect," Roland Barthes starts with the question of description as a way of getting to the heart of what constitutes realism: "Is everything in narrative significant, and if not, if insignificant stretches subsist in the narrative syntagm, what is the significance of this insignificance?"[11] Description tells what is there, as if it had to do so because what was there was there. Aesthetic realism, what Barthes calls "modern realism" is a mode in which representations are "justified by their referent alone": "The *having-been-there* of things is a sufficient principle of speech."[12] The prop is the cinema's agent of "having been there." In the context of a realist cinema, the prop is used to figure contingency itself.[13] And realism consists in the assemblage of props into an image of contingency. Props seem to be there with an effortlessness that belies the effort involved in dragging them there—onto the set, in front of the camera.

Recalling the invisible labor that has dragged these props before the camera of Welles's cinematographer Gregg Toland compels us to read into the closing sequence of *Citizen Kane* a sense of the prop's necessity. Necessity, here, is not ontological or god-given, but is simply what is required for the film—the need that caused the prop to be placed just there and not somewhere else. Cinematic realism consists in the careful erasure of the labors that have been expended to make the film look realistic, like what we see in the world. By looking like the world, so the story goes, the film allows us to forget that we are looking at it, and thus settle into the comforts of illusionism (as dangerous as they are pleasurable, according to many traditions in critical theory). The prop, therefore, is also always a sign of labor that is under erasure, and its erasure allows us to relax into our consumption of the film. We do not see or think about the labor of the person who made the prop, or the labor of the person who positioned it in a particular place on the set. But there is something about the prop's material there-ness (or having-been-there-ness) that nags at this cozy viewing position. We look at the prop with a sort of double vision: "Oh, that just happened to be there!" and "Oh, I know someone put that there!" In this sense the realist prop (or the prop in service to realism) incarnates in miniature the disavowal that, according to Metz, structures the film viewing experience as a whole. Contrarily, in the case of the continuity error—we might think of the famous paper coffee cup that was left on set in an episode of the final season of *Game of Thrones* (HBO 2011–19)—our response to the image of the mislaid object would be "Oh, someone must have left that there!" The effect is a painful rupturing of the surface of the fiction, and yet, the disavowal continues: we keep watching. Is the coffee cup a prop, even though it ought not to be there and threatens to undo or disrupt the work of all the other elements at work in the image? In an important sense it isn't: The prop should subtend, not destroy, the fiction. And yet, insofar as it is an object set before and captured by the camera, its unruly appearance (like a hole in the screen of the image) offers up the negative truth content of all the other props which are well-behaved and doing their jobs. So in some sense, if it is not a prop, per se, our ability to see it depends on the regime of prophood whose laws it momentarily perverts.

In narrative fiction filmmaking, the prop is a part of the diegetic world. Frequently, it has merely been borrowed from "the world" and deposited in the diegetic world. But the prop is not just part of that world, one of its divisible units. There is no diegetic world without props, unless we were to imagine a fictional film consisting entirely of close-ups of the human face shot against a completely blank wall, or a film consisting only of a voice-over with an entirely blank screen. Dreyer's *The Passion of Joan of Arc* (1928) comes close to what is described in the first instance, and while not entirely fictional, Andy Warhol's *Blow Job* (1964), might as well, while Derek Jarman's *Blue* (1993) might exemplify the second instance. Putting such hypothetical limit cases to one side, we can assert the prop's ontogenetic function in cinema. It is not merely decorative ground to the human figure, or a kind of filler that fleshes out the fictional world. Its function is more primary—or, going further, more primordial.

Props therefore need to be there and are there—and there they are. Their function is to efface: thereness is all. In being there, in existing below the threshold of purposiveness they also exist just below the threshold of meaning. Props are metonymic, we might be led to believe, if we follow this train of thought. They are horizontal, they are to hand, ready to be picked up, held, sat on, broken, burned, eaten, and abused. But we can only persist along this train of thought for so long before we remind ourselves that cinema's capacity for symbolization and metaphorization is also a matter of prop management. If we think of cinema's most outrageous attempts to create a line of flight out of horizontality, contiguity, metonymy—out of realism, that is—and into the verticality of metaphor, these will often involve the mobilization (the heavy-handed radical manipulation, we might say) of a prop.

Think of Sergei Eisenstein's use of a mechanical peacock in the famous sequence of *October* (1927) that follows Kerensky's endlessly protracted ascent of the staircase of the Winter Palace as a succession of intertitles name the various titles that this false revolutionary, this figure of unbearable compromise, has given to himself: ("Dictator, Minister of the Army, Minister of the Navy, Prime Minister" and then the caustic "Etc..., etc..., etc..."). At the top of stairs, after he has been met and greeted by various functionaries of the tsarist state who recognize him as a useful stooge, close-ups of his body (the backs of his calves bound in leather boots, his leather-gloved left hand clutching his right-hand glove tightly behind his back) are intercut with close-ups of what looks like a metallic (gold?) peacock. First it does not move. Then, in successive shots, as the film cuts back and forth between the details of Kerensky's fetish gear and this gaudy fetish object, the peacock begins to whir into mechanical motion. It is some kind of automaton, something controlled by another force—like Kerensky himself. Expanding its tail feathers to their fullest height and breadth, the peacock twirls around (about five times, across as many shots, if we count correctly) to present its ass to us. Next the film cuts to a shot of Kerensky in front of the doors of the imperial chambers that, in imitation of the peacock's flaunting of its inorganic golden backside, fling themselves open, one, two, three times, across three shots, as Kerensky and members of his retinue walk on through. Finally, the doors shut—magically moving on their own, like the peacock—and the film cuts back to the peacock, which twirls around again, mechanically cocking its mechanical head.[14]

The prop here—the peacock, a tsarist tchotchke, we presume—is famously the ground of a metaphorical comparison. But it is interesting that (to our knowledge) no one has faced the issue of the prop as the ground, the helpless vehicle, of this metaphor. The peacock as a figure, of course, is multivalent and elusive in its signification: an icon of vanity, an attribute of Juno, a figure of watchfulness. Vanity would seem to be most germane to Eisenstein's comparison of two mostly unlike things. But the propness of the metaphor, that a prop is one of the two terms being yoked into the metaphorical relation, is perhaps even more apt. What is Kerensky other than a prop—a puppet, a plaything, a bit of property owned by the tsarist regime? In other words, he is just like the peacock in many respects, well beyond the abstract connotation of vanity. But then this is where things get sticky, if we are going to try to think of the prop as the substance or vehicle of metaphor. If metaphor demands the comparison of two things that are not contiguously related so as to force an awareness of a relation that did not at first seem obviously available to us, then the peacock as metaphorical prop might not carry us up to the verticality that we desire. Peacocks cannot fly very far or very well, and although we do not know where in the Winter Palace this peacock, as a bit of gaudy decor, might have been found, it seems thoroughly grounded in a contiguous relationship to Kerensky and the other denizens of this seat of royal imperial power. The prop has let us down. The peacock's feathers shimmied and shook so as to lift us up into the heights of metaphorization, but the peacock turns its ass so as to shit us back out onto the plains of contiguity, the steppes of a kind of wild realism. Eisenstein's rigorous, abstract, slightly hysterical cutting (what he called "intellectual montage") constitutes an intense attempt to prop the prop into a vertical relationship to meaning. The camera, it seems, on one hand, can hunt down or chance upon or curatorially isolate a thing and electrify it with the attention of its mechanical gaze. (This is the magnification of which Epstein speaks.) But, on the other hand, the prop is a kind of deadweight that seems always to want to fall back down into the world where things lie next to one another and just are.

Inside the symbolic abstractions that result from Eisenstein's coercion of the prop into meaning, we sense, in other words, the reality and the materiality on which meaning rests itself. The prop's often dense reality is a hard surface from which the film launches itself into complex signification. Filmmaking practices born in or by periods of historical crisis seem to bring these dynamics into view, often under the banner of realism, although not the realism of *Citizen Kane*'s exquisite repletion. Eisenstein's is a highly patterned realism—a realism of social stereotypes that are embodied by over-particularized faces, and of real objects that give body to abstract ideological arguments.

The prop, perhaps, could be a way of renovating or rewriting historiographic and theoretical accounts of cinematic realism. Italian neorealism—the film movement (or period in film history) that followed Italy's emergence from not only World War II but also twenty years of Fascist rule—offers perhaps the most urgent and most influential mobilization of the problem or practice of realism in the history of cinema.

Debates about what neorealism is or isn't are too complex—and often too tedious—for us to consider here, but what we can say, and in the spirit of perhaps being able to say something new, is that some of the most celebrated and most canonical neorealist films offer an enlivened and enlarged use of props as narrative structuring devices and as anchors to the everyday reality of immiseration and its (potential, frail) redemption that are neorealism's persistent themes. Neorealism's greatest (commercial) success, Bicycle Thieves (Vittorio De Sica, 1948) gestures eponymously toward its most famous prop—one glimpsed, however, only fleetingly, in the film's beginning and concluding passages. The stolen bicycle's structuring absence motivates the film's meandering narrative development. The theft of the bicycle shapes the film's movements and its narrative temporality. A thought experiment: What sort of film might Bicycle Thieves have been if its protagonist's bike had not been stolen? Would we have followed Antonio Ricci (Lamberto Maggiorani) across his entire working day, plastering up posters that advertise the imminent release of Gilda? If so, Bicycle Thieves could have been more "boring" than the film De Sica actually made. Or would the celerity afforded him by his unstolen bicycle allowed him to get into other types of eventful trouble—marital indiscretion? a brush with the law? a trip outside Rome? But then, perhaps, the film would not have answered the imperatives of neorealism itself. No one agrees *exactly* on what these imperatives are, but it may be fair to say that there is a consensus that neorealism should: focus on the representation of the small events of ordinary life, lived by ordinary people; use (or pretend to use) the real people, places, and things of the world in mounting its representation; align stylistic and formal strategies to the necessities of the representational content. So Ricci must move rather more haphazardly in and around Rome, hoping to recover what has been taken from him. Sometimes he moves too quickly, at others he seems barely able to move at all. At the root of everything is the missing bicycle, which, ironically, was already missing at the film's beginning. When Ricci is offered a job putting up posters, the only question he is asked at the employment office is if he has a bicycle. He does and he doesn't: His bicycle, we find out later, is in the pawn shop. But he lies to get the job, then enlists his wife in hocking their marital linens in order to redeem the bicycle. The scene in which the couple turn over their laundered neatly folded bed things to the man behind the desk at the pawn shop is itself a condensation of propness. As his assistant climbs a ladder to deposit the sheets on a high shelf, the camera tilts to allow us a vision of hundreds and hundreds of other bolts of bedding: These props stand in for the impoverished multitudes whose actual persons the film allows us only fleetingly to glimpse at various points.

The missing bicycle—the missing prop—grounds the film in the concreteness of its historical horizon while also fundamentally catalyzing its aesthetic experimentation. Robert Gordon writes that "the bicycle distills Antonio's predicament into a single, simple image"; it is "a resonant symbol within the complex symbolic economy of the film" and "an emblem of the particular moment of historical transition at which Antonio's world—Italy, 1948—stands."[15] And Giuliana Minghelli argues that "with the disappearance of the bike ... the story loosens, becomes episodic; time drags to a virtual standstill amid the many digressions during the erratic Sunday search through Rome."[16] The bicycle's narrative and aesthetic function grows out of the lived reality of postwar Rome's historical terrain. Rome was a city whose poor—like Ricci— had long been displaced to the city's periphery; and it was a city poor in public transportation. We could say that the bike is insufficiently symbolic, insofar as it substitutes itself for nothing. Its humility is a vehicle for the film's articulation of the stakes of being poor, dispossessed, displaced, and derided in Rome in 1948.[17]

One of neorealism's most powerful aesthetic strategies is its focus on the minor, the overlooked, the interstitial—those events that do not register as events—at least not until observed by the camera and projected on-screen. *Umberto D.*, another film directed by De Sica from a screenplay written by Cesare Zavattini, and released in 1952, follows the depressing attempts of its eponymous petit bourgeois protagonist (Carlo Battisti), an old age pensioner living in a rented room, to stay alive and stay housed. The film's most celebrated and certainly its most singular scene depicts Maria (Maria Pia Casilio), a live-in domestic servant working in the house of Umberto D.'s landlady, as she goes about her morning routine of making coffee for her mistress. In this scene, time stands nearly still, or rather is divided and subdivided into so many tiny moments. Waking up, putting on her slippers, taking a drink of water straight from the tap, filling the coffee grinder with beans, bracing the device in her lap, against her abdomen, and slowly doing the job of grinding the coffee, while simultaneously trying to reach her foot to close the door. These are Maria's wordless actions, and they take up a little more than four minutes of screen time: little more than a sustained blip in the film's duration, but an enormity in terms of their resonance—infinite riches in a little room. It could be seen as an exercise in the miniature, but its discrete bracketing off from the rest of the film (to which it is only loosely connected in any thematic sense or in relation to the plot) enlarges its presence for us, even if its significance remains almost completely opaque. Time stands still: Nothing happens. But time moves on, inexorably: By the scene's end, the coffee is ground. Everything has happened. The grinder itself and Maria's practiced but nonetheless rather clumsy manipulation of it absorb our attention and measure the time of the scene; each circular movement of her hand grinds out the scene's micro-temporal duration, while also grinding the coffee, converting raw material into a comestible beverage. This little prop is the still-moving center and the fulcrum of the ambitions of a film aesthetic that seeks to valorize the under-visualized conditions and experiences—in many cases buttressed by gendered, domestic, reproductive labor—that constitute life itself. Bazin writes of this "wonderful sequence" that "De Sica and Zavattini attempt to divide the event into still smaller events and these into events smaller still, to the extreme limits of our capacity to perceive them in time."[18] The prop is the mechanical heart of this phenomenological undertaking.

Bazin attributes to De Sica and Zavattini a desire "to make cinema the asymptote of reality" so that "it should ultimately be life itself that becomes spectacle."[19] Bazin could feel confident saying all of this about Zavattini and De Sica because these were things, as Bazin notes in the same essay, that they said themselves. In an essay in which we find some of the most hyperbolic articulations of the aesthetic and ideological ambitions of neorealism, "Some Ideas on the Cinema" (first published in 1952, the same year *Umberto D.* was released),

Zavattini argues that "there must be no gap between life and what is on the screen."[20] The device for closing this gap turns out to be the prop, as we discover in the example Zavattini gives for his dream of sublating cinema and life:

> A woman goes to a shop to buy a pair of shoes. The shoes cost 7,000 lire. [Note: This figure would amount to a little over $100 in 2023.] The woman tries to bargain. The scene lasts perhaps two minutes. I must make a two-hour film. What do I do?
>
> I analyse the fact in all its constituent elements, in its "before," in its "after," in its contemporaneity. The fact creates its own fiction, in its own particular sense.
>
> The woman is buying the shoes. What is her son doing at the same moment? What are people doing in India that could have some relation to this fact of the shoes? The shoes cost 7,000 lire. How did the woman happen to have 7,000 lire? How hard did she work for them, what do they represent for her?
>
> And the bargaining shopkeeper, who is he? What relationship has developed between these two human beings? What do they mean, what interests are they defending, as they bargain? The shopkeeper also has two sons, who eat and speak: do you want to know what they are saying? Here they are, in front of you ...
>
> The question is, to be able to fathom the real correspondences between facts and their process of birth, to discover what lies beneath them.
>
> Thus to analyse "buying a pair of shoes" in such a way opens us to a vast and complex world, rich in importance and values, in its practical, social, economic,

> psychological motives. Banality disappears because each
> moment is really charged with responsibility. Every moment is infinitely rich. Banality never existed.[21]

What Zavattini describes is probably the greatest unmade neorealist film. And at the center of this imagined film, a pair of unbought shoes. The conceit of this two-minute scene from which two hours of duration will flow is a prop. The anecdote makes sense—perhaps only makes sense—in the economy of scarcity that was Rome in the immediate aftermath of World War II. The economy of scarcity, however, trains attention on the way in which the prop—the pair of shoes, an ordinary commodity, one woven into and out of the vast networks of capitalist exchange—condenses a manifold abundance of narrative and aesthetic possibilities. Neorealism names and endows us with a model of filmmaking and film theory in which the smallest unit of the material world discloses the vastness of social relations in capitalist modernity.

In the anecdote of the shoes, Zavattini gesturally elaborates a claim that De Sica had made earlier in an interview in 1948 about *Bicycle Thieves*: "My aim is to identify the dramatic in everyday situations, the marvelous in the minor chronicle [*cronaca*], indeed in the most minor chronicle, which most consider worn-out material."[22] These everyday situations are found events—narrative *objets trouvés*. In their found-ness they are bound to the question of the non-professional actors, discovered by directors and casting agents on the streets of Rome, who populate neorealist films. Although the nonprofessional actor's dominance in neorealism is something of a myth, it is still the case that Lamberto Maggiorani, who played

Ricci in *Bicycle Thieves*, was in fact a Roman factory worker.[23] The non-idealized physicality of an actor like Maggiorani imports into the film the authenticity of his physical and social being. Even if his imperfect acting may create a small fissure or tear in the fiction's fabric, his found, organically ready-made, non-artificial being roots the film in the real in a way that supersedes questions of absorption, skill, or fictional plausibility. The found prop acts in the same way. Ricci's bicycle, for instance, operates like Maggiorani's body: at once made up and a part of the material and social reality of the streets of Rome in 1948. Nothing is more real than this body or this bicycle; and neither is more real than anything else that could have been scooped up from the same streets in the same year. Neorealism's influence endows the global new waves that followed (self-consciously or not) in its wake with a radically enlarged vision of the power and possibility of the prop when placed in the service of revolutionary realism.

There is little written about the "influence" of Italian neorealism on the revolutionary cinemas that emerged in Africa in the period of decolonization. Of course, even to talk in terms of influence is to repeat the logics of centers and peripheries, originals and imitations that have structured colonialist thinking. Recent scholarship has acknowledged that "there is little evidence of any direct influence of Italian cinema in Africa," while also taking seriously the ways in which filmmakers in Latin America and Africa "built on and developed aspects of neorealism while rejecting others."[24] One way of taking up the relation, of sensing both lines of affiliation, correlation (rather than hierarchical influence) and dissonance, would be to foreground the way props are both found and put to work in both neorealism and African anti-colonial cinema, specifically in the case of Senegalese cinema.

Ousmane Sembène's landmark first film *La noire de . . . / Black Girl* (1966) was based on a short story Sembène wrote, which was originally published in *Presence Africaine* in 1961; its narrative was drawn—akin to the tradition of the neorealist *cronaca*—from a newspaper item he read about, a real event that occurred in 1958.[25] This newspaper story itself appears as a prop in the film's conclusion, giving a concretely visualized specificity to the doubly fictionalized story that has up to that point been fleshed out in terms of generality and genre. The film represents a mobilization of neorealism's prioritizing of the prop in its centrality to narrative signification, as an engine of eventfulness and meaning production. In its movement between flashbacks and the film's enunciating present, *Black Girl* depicts the tragic fate of a young Senegalese woman Diouana, played by Mbissine Thérèse Diop, who is hired by a French family, first in Dakar as a nanny of three children, and then in Antibes as a domestic servant in their thoroughly midcentury modern and middle-class apartment. As an isolated migrant worker in despair over her alienated working conditions, she commits suicide, a tragic act of refusal and protest against her exploitation by her French employers.

Sembène's strategic use of props—the way he forces them to circulate from character to character in the diegesis—reflexively narrates the circulatory networks of consumer capitalism and forms of neocolonial expropriation. Through props Sembène expresses the alienating and oppressive effects of neocolonialism in the relationships and economic exigencies of a post-independence Senegal. Sembène describes his use of objects as a mode of sociohistorical referentiality: "Film language requires a certain punctuation and some objects allow me to punctuate my films."[26] The grammatically significatory work of props, in particular the film's centerpiece prop, the traditional African mask that Diouana buys from a neighborhood boy in Dakar and gives to her employer, "Madame" (Anne-Marie Jelinek), animates the symbolic and metaphorical economy of the film's exposition of oppressive systems. The mask's prop value is bound up in its status not only as a signifier of cultural heritage in the world but also as a vehicle and index of power relations across class, race, and gender in the film. The mask is torn from its context in Dakar where it exists as an everyday object, although one also endowed with a powerful cultural specificity and intended, potential ritual function. Once given by Diouana (sincerely) to her white employers, it becomes an exoticized *objet d'art* in the French home, a self-consciously displayed token of cultural authenticity that declares its elsewhereness, as well as its newly imposed domestication. The mask's circulation echoes Diouana's own shifting positionality inside economies of aspiration, labor, and racialized coercion. Placed first in the employer's Dakar home, which is replete with many other relics and traditional ritual objects picked up, we assume, along their travels, the mask sits as merely one specimen among many others like it. When later we see it hanging in her employers' notably smaller (and for Diouna, starkly claustrophobic) apartment in Antibes, its looming, isolated presence on the otherwise bare wall announces it as haunting, suggestive of oblique threat. Seduced by promises of a life of consumerist plenitude in France and expecting to continue her role as childminder, Diouana takes the job in

Antibes, offered to her under false pretenses. She becomes ensnared in a daily grind of unending, deadening housework, as she toils under the constant surveillance of the punitive Madame. The woman of the house's social status now seems to directly rely on her ostentatious display of Diouana to the white, French guests who come to lunch, for which Diouana has been instructed to prepare the traditionally Senegalese dish of rice with mafé. She notes to herself in the voice-over narration that rice was never eaten by her employers when in Dakar, suggesting that the cultural specificity of cuisine is a mobile signifier of class standing vis-à-vis the strains of fading empire for the French couple, who are now in the position to need to reassert their distinction and cosmopolitanism. The continuum created between Diouana's labor, her subjection, and her racialization is tantamount to her status as tacit possession of her employers. She and the mask ironize and mirror each other's existence in the house, as Sembène invites the viewer to consider the many forms of misalignment and realignment between them as figured by the white employers. Diop's performance is intentionally reticent, withdrawn, inexpressive, mask-like. We are only privy to Diouana's feelings via the film's use of first-person voice-over, which is paradoxically presented in a French narration, a compromise held against the narration's suggestion that she speaks little French.

The conflict between Diouana and her employers and her resistance to her subordination escalate once she fully realizes how thoroughly she is held captive in the white-walled Antibes flat, where she has been consigned to indentured servitude, stripped of her agency, and denied any autonomous space or free time beyond the antiseptic walls of the apartment, or an occasional trip to the grocer or butcher. Diouana is continually subjected to Madame's racist abuse. She is told not to wear the stylish hand-me-downs (a black and white polka dotted sleeveless dress and black slingback pumps) that Madame had given her in Dakar. Madame's guests appraise her exotic foreignness; one male guest goes so far as to kiss her without her permission. When the oldest son of Madame's three children abruptly (and without explanation) appears in Antibes, Madame's abuse increases, and Diouana begins quietly to rebel by shirking her housekeeping, sleeping in, and ignoring Madame's demands. In a dramatic scene of revolt, Diouana reclaims the mask from the wall, in order to reappropriate it in her movement toward the restitution of her integrity, worth, and identity.

The mask's shifting semiotic play as a prop condenses the film's critique of colonialism's *longue durée*—as well as its history of extracting value from cultural objects and living human beings. In an interview Sembène speaks of the mask as not a "mystical symbol" but a "symbol of unity and identity and the recuperation of our culture," yet he also acknowledges that the mask was, at the time of the film's production, a contemporary commodity, an "article for export for tourists."[27] The prop here bears a heavy semiotic surplus and narrative function diegetically: It is gift, cultural artifact, art object, decor, and a figure of possession and dispossession. Finally it is an abstracted sign that enacts its own revenge by haunting, in the film's concluding section. After a disconsolate Diouana slits her own throat in the bath in a final devastating act of refusal, the man of the house ("Monsieur," played by Robert Fontaine) returns to Dakar to give back Diouana's belongings, including the mask, to her mother. Along with these bitter remnants, he attempts to ply her with a handful of cash. Diouana's mother stoically refuses this hollow gesture. The little boy who had originally given the mask to Diouana regains the object, and trails after Monsieur wearing it. Its abstraction functions as an open signifier, an otherworldly vengeance. Now manifest as specter of death and unearthly restitution, Monsieur is chased by its ghostly force, as if it will possess him against his will. The mask's shuttling between material specificity and abstraction endows it with a rich polysemy that is one of the film's main sources of anticolonial critique.

Yet an exclusive focus on the mask overlooks the way Sembène marshals it in relation to other props that are imbricated with it in circuits of labor, exchange, and value. Diouana's articles of clothing, her shoes in particular, are loaded signifiers, marking her dereliction of duties as she casts them off later in the film. On the morning in which Diouana's resistance first announces itself, she refuses to wake early to serve breakfast, and is forcefully roused and harangued by Madame to get to work. Ignoring Madame, she moves at her own pace, observing her own sense of ritual as she readies herself for the morning and combs out her natural hair, which has been covered by a wig in Antibes. She eventually emerges from her room in a dress and her black pumps. Madame insists she remove the shoes: "Don't forget you're a maid!" she barks. Diouna, framed in long shot, positioned between the mask on the wall in the background behind her and Madame sitting on the sofa in the foreground, looks back. In silence, she languidly removes her shoes, leaving them in the middle of the floor for Madame to clear away, thus refusing her duties as housekeeper. Technically, while being worn on the actor's body, shoes function as costume, but once taken off, they assume the status of props. Diouana's shoes, now palpable as props, become a burden for her employers, the property masters. Their lability is not unlike that of the mask: once decorative, objects of desire, projection, or self-fashioning, now a source of bitter contention. Cast off, bound to a gesture of resistance, the becoming-prop of the shoes is also their becoming subverted tool against Diouana's oppression.

We do not reckon carefully enough with the function of these props in *Black Girl* if we do not take on the task of reading their polemical obviousness in the film. Sembène directs—even over-directs—our attention to the mask. Its demonstrative diegetic symbolism, its hypervisibility on the wall, its movement back and forth between Dakar and Antibes, between black and white owners, and finally its radical reappropriation (as symbol and as weapon): These dimensions of its use cannot be missed by attentive spectators in their attempt to understand the film. The film's parting shot presents the gaze of the mask at the camera, in direct address to the spectator. The boy slowly removes it to reveal his face beneath, as credits roll. In this final insistence on the mask's overwhelming centrality to the film, Sembène invites the viewer to consider this prop-object, and to consider all the life, labor, and history that enfolds and sustains it, as the kernel of the film's formal and political intervention. To watch the film at all is to respond to its demand to think about its central prop. The mask as prop is made to do all sorts of narrative, symbolic, and semiotic labor across the film. In turn, the mask demands labor from us: "Interpret me," it demands of us. In this sense, the mask functions in a manner that might be productively

compared to that of Rosebud, the sled in *Citizen Kane*. While glimpses of Rosebud are coyly offered to us in the beginning movements of the film, we mostly do not see it, nor do we recognize it when we do. It is not until the very end of the film, when the camera stealthily swoops down on the sled just as it is thrown into the burning maw of the furnace, that we are able to marry signifier to signified and thus, perhaps, solve the film's epistemological provocation. The close-up on the sled is an obvious gesture; the flagrancy of its exhibitionism is commensurate with the hokiness of its entire conceit as shibboleth-cum-narrative catalyst.

Child's sled, golden peacock, stolen bicycle, ritual mask. Realism, in all its modalities and across the entire arc of film history, depends on the prop to do its work. And for the spectator, the prop becomes the condensed object of hermeneutic labor. The prop works (or is put to work, is an instrument of work) for and in the film. It works on us; we work with it. The prop makes worlds appear and furnishes the world's appearance. It also justly lends itself as a tool for the unmaking of the world's infinitely cruel injustice.

5

The Prop and the Performer

Beth is a beleaguered young lawyer who drives four hours away from her regular job to teach education law in a small town called Belfry, Montana. In a scene set in a diner, Jamie, with no food of her own to distract her, watches as Beth eats a meal of burger and fries. Jamie, played by Lily Gladstone, is a ranch hand who has shown up for Beth's evening class. Beth, played by Kristen Stewart, in this seemingly throwaway moment, performs a bit of prop-business both subtle and disarming in neo-neo-realist filmmaker Kelly Reichardt's *Certain Women* (2016). The scene begins with Beth having already sliced her burger in half. Beth takes a bite, then picks up what food-service workers sometimes call a "roll-up," or what patrons of a diner like this might call a "place setting": flatware tightly wrapped inside a paper napkin. Beth clearly must have already withdrawn the knife from the napkin in order to cut the burger, but she goes on to do something that is both prosaic and bizarre: She uses the roll-up as if it were an unfolded napkin. She presses the napkin, which

still contains spoon and fork, to dab daintily the corner of her mouth. This prop—the roll-up—is quotidian, familiar, banal—something found in any greasy spoon. This tiny but arresting gesture is repeated a few moments later, as Beth chews, talks, and explains the duress of her long commute. Jamie, we begin to realize, is smitten with Beth. In her handling of this ordinary object, Stewart (as Beth) makes conspicuous this prop via what seems to be an improvisational gesture. The roll-up announces the modest customs of middle-American foodways and allows the opportunity for the performer to articulate something about the character she plays. Beth must make haste; she needs to keep moving, and her impatience is communicated through her strange handling of what would otherwise be a generic, forgettable prop, something that might ordinarily escape notice entirely. Beth cannot entertain Jamie's offer of friendship to her momentary companion. The tightly bound confection of paper napkin and industrial flatware stands in for the emotional tenor of this nascent relationship between two strangers. What pressures—temporal, psychic, material—make unrolling a napkin and using it appropriately a seemingly impossible task? This minor scene is emblematic of Vsevolod Pudovkin's notion of the "expressive object." Stewart's fugitive moments of prop play offer deeper insight into Beth's character, as well as into Stewart's peculiarly diffident, slouchy performance style. Pudovkin insists on the power of inanimate objects in the cinema when he argues that "an object, linked to an actor, can bring shades of his state of emotion to external expression so deeply as no gesture or mimicry could ever express them conditionally."[1] Undemonstrative and mundane, the roll-up—this tightly wrapped bundle of serviceware—unwraps a view of film performance's entwinement with the cinematic prop's necessity.

The relationship of props to the embodied performer, the integral role they play in the gestural labor of the actor, is threaded through our entire discussion, but it is worthwhile here to tease out the investments and entrenched relations between performance and prop value. Cinema's foundational fascination with bodily movement entails a frequent lingering on the prop and the role of objects; this preoccupation is noticeable across the history of cinema, from pre-cinematic motion studies and early cinema's development as a narrational medium, all the way through actor training exercises in various schools of performance, including The Method and its multiple tributaries and variants. In numerous attempts to account for the essence of cinema, theorists suggest that the capture of corporeal movement entails a grappling with things that is central to the prop's circulation through the diegesis, and thus to the unfolding of the diegesis itself. As plot vector, currency, relational mediator, agent of memory, appendage or illuminator of character, and dramatic catalyst, the prop buttresses and expands the very energies of cinematic narration and the articulation of character. The hands that hold and grab props set fields of activity in motion and generate horizons of narrativity. The prop's status as an expressive resource is bound up with the performer's bodily activity. In his account of film acting, James Naremore suggests that "actors need to touch things" by necessity, and this necessity of handling the prop world is a vital means of producing screen presence, key to the construction of a coherent fictional self. He further notes that "part of the actor's job is to keep objects under expressive control, letting them become signifiers of feeling."[2] Concerned with how the border between prop and performer breaks down or becomes porous, Naremore points to elements of screen performances, from Charlie Chaplin's cane to Barbara Stanwyck's subtly wielded handkerchief in the tearful ending of *Stella Dallas* (King Vidor, 1937), as examples of how acting techniques extend from an intensified relation between prop and character. In their different generic registers Chaplin's comedic hyperbole and Stanwyck's melodramatic realism demonstrate how prop work generates the gestural flow between action and expression.

Chaplin's work as a performer demands greater attention in order to understand how props, in the slapstick tradition, animate the causal chain of the comic gag. In *The Pawnshop* (1916) we see the articulation of an ethos of prop-ness as the spring that sets Chaplin's comedy in motion. The prop is crucial to his Tramp persona's critique of the terms of capitalist modernity. The Tramp is hired to work in a pawnshop, a site of value appraisal which also becomes the testing ground for the limits of objects and commodities when they cross paths with the deranging principles of the performer's disorderly chaos, famously the Midas touch of Chaplinian contingency. Chaplin's hands pervert the functionality of objects and redirect them from their intended use. Transformed through gags, a clothes wringer becomes a dish dryer, a donut becomes a dumbbell, a ladder becomes a cage and a weapon. In one of the film's most prolonged and intricate gags, an alarm clock morphs through Chaplin's handling: It is tapped and palpated like a mechanical patient, next inspected like an open can of sardines, and finally dissected like a frog in formaldehyde. Eventually, the Tramp pulls out the insides of the clock as though they are slippery entrails. Once reduced to incoherent uselessness on the pawnshop counter, the clock's parts begin to move in insect-like animation. The Tramp uses an oilcan as if it were insect repellent in order to stop the crawling screws and springs in their tracks, before sweeping the dissected parts back into the bewildered customer's hat and sending him on his way. Noel Carroll describes this comedic sight gag as a form of "mimed metaphor" in which the prop is a vehicle for the "play of interpretive incongruity."[3] Yet we might think further about how *The Pawnshop* represents the prop's motility at work in Chaplin's aesthetic sensibility: The prop is an agent of metaphorization, but simultaneously it is the very grounds of the performance. The exchangeability and convertibility of the prop enable it to act as vehicle for performative virtuosity, on the scale of what Lesley Stern calls the histrionic function of cinematic gesture. In Chaplin's performance the misuse of the prop unleashes a chain of signifying and figural transformations that undo the prop's initial and normative diegetic function and thus usher it out of the domain of literality. Chaplin's propped performances initiate and sustain processes of chaotically rigorous transformation that underscore the alchemical nature of the performer's power to translate the prop's properties into a strange new idiom. In Chaplin's cinema the control of expressive feeling through the use of the prop that Naremore describes is directed toward an undoing of control itself, a sort of laborious unmaking that points to the arbitrary status of the prop's normative utility or use value in narrative fiction.

Seemingly far away from Chaplin's acrobatic hyperbole of slapstick prop-play, realist modes of performance place the prop in a quotidian register. In a famous scene in Elia Kazan's *On the Waterfront* (1954), the improvisatory nature of the moment in which Marlon Brando takes Eva Marie Saint's glove out of her hand and then puts it on his own, in an act of eccentric and urgent courtship and reconnection, might be seen as a precursor to Stewart's performance, in the hamburger scene, of the involution of the self in a state of precarity. In the realist and dramatic acting traditions known as The Method, Lee Strasberg's adaptation and interpretation of the teaching of Konstantin Stanislavsky, the prop plays a foundational role. Strasberg's introductory and most well-known training exercise, frequently referred to as the "coffee cup" or "morning drink" exercise, activated what he termed "sense memories" through the faculties of touch, taste, and smell.[4] The morning drink exercise invited the rehearsing actor to establish a physical familiarity with a coffee cup, to track its shape, weight, and feeling in one's hands. This handling of the cup triggered the resuscitation of a range of sensual experiences: the heat of the cup, the smell and taste of the coffee inside it. These actions were next performed by the actor, but this time without the cup. In variations on the exercise, the group in training would be asked to recognize what was being handled by the mimetic gestures of the actor with an absent object in their performed possession. The spectral object, despite its not-there-ness, nevertheless animates the actor's performance. This strange, ghostly comportment demonstrates the prop's indispensability to the techniques, psychic operations, and training regimes that underpin the actor's work in narrative cinema. To see the phantom prop, the absent coffee cup through the actor's performance of its fictional presence offers another iteration of what we call prop value, that quality of the object that enables the performance to "work" to produce realism. The prop—both a spectral vessel and an animating presence in the scene of Method performance—thus activates a whole range of mental and corporeal operations in the actor's practice. The phantom prop's grounding of performance might also be glimpsed in the contemporary domain of a digital production regime within which actors must act against a green screen and interact with objects and beings who are not there, or not yet there, and who will be made present through CGI.

Method acting's radical cathexis of the prop bears late season fruit in surprising contexts—in filmmaking and performance practices that might seem the antithesis of Method authenticity, such as the unlikely arena of the teen sex comedy of the 1980s. *Risky Business* (Paul Brickman, 1983) is, if not at the origin point of this genre, then surely its most celebrated iteration. At its center, of course, we find Tom Cruise, that most durable star commodity, who, according to numerous anecdotal accounts of the film's production "became" Tom Cruise in this film.[5] But Tom Cruise became Tom Cruise not so much in this film in general, but in its most iconic and imitated scene, a mere one minute of screen time that occurs ten minutes into the film's duration.

Cruise plays Joel Goodson, an allegorically named character, apparently the only child of upper-middle-class parents with whom he resides in a Colonial Revival two-story house in suburban Chicago. (This is a setting one associates with a film like *Ordinary People* [Robert Redford, 1980] or *Ferris Bueller's Day Off* [John Hughes, 1986.]) He is good looking, of above-average scholastic aptitude (we learn he has scored just below 1200 on his SATs), and a virgin. His parents are pushy, seemingly comfortable in their blandly but expensively decorated home, but at the same time, neurotically overinvested in its luxuries: There is a Porsche in the garage, a fancy hi-fi tastefully stored in a wooden cupboard, and a Steuben crystal egg, roughly the size of a small football, that sits in the middle of the mantel. The parents' only salient characterological trait is, actually, their precious concern for these commodities. Are they "new money," we might wonder, and therefore a bit too attached to these things? The film does not tell us, but in telling us that these things preoccupy them, it grants itself the occasion to dwell on them—the car, the stereo, the crystal egg—and thus to make manifest its visual and narrative investment in its props in a more general sense. When Joel's parents leave him alone for the weekend, their main advice has more to do with care for the suburban estate than care for him: "Don't forget to water the plants around the patio, and the ficus in the dining room." When concern for Joel is expressed, it is primarily via the $125 that, while bidding him farewell at the airport, Joel's mother offers him ($50 for food—"Which should be more than enough"—$50 for "emergencies" and "another $25 just in case").

The scene of the parents' departure begins in the Goodson home and occasions our first glimpse of its interior. Throughout, the camera maintains a point-of-view cinematography reminiscent of *Lady of the Lake* (Robert Montgomery, 1947), in which Joel's parents seem to address him by addressing the handheld camera, which bobs and weaves as if responding to them. The camera-as-Joel (we hear his mumbled reactions to their litany of advice and warnings) follows Mr. Goodson from the kitchen, where the scene begins, to the living room, where Joel's father admonishes him against the misuse of his hi-fi, and in particular its equalizer: "If you can't use it properly, you're not to use it all—my house, my rules." As this line is spoken, the camera glides towards the mantel above the fireplace to frame in close-up the aforementioned crystal egg, flanked by a pair of matching brass candlesticks. As the camera draws even closer to the mantelpiece, the egg is briefly framed entirely on its own. What is this senseless, expensive-looking globular shard of translucence? Given that we are inhabiting Joel's point of view, the shot's brief emphasis on this tony tchotchke presents something of an enigma. Are we to believe it is of special concern to Joel? Or is it a symbolic condensation—both metonymic and metaphoric—of the Goodsons' class position, their curatorial concern with their possessions, their concern with Joel's good behavior, his SAT scores, and his application to Princeton (which, along with the whereabouts of the egg, is one of the film's running jokes and sources of narrative anxiety). Their objectification of Joel's qualities renders him hardly more than an enfleshed and sentient crystal egg: decorative, modern, isolated, expensively banal, nearly perfect—and flanked by two more traditional presences (the brass candlesticks) that have little to do with him, apart from their mere proximity in the confines of the Goodson home.

Once Joel is finally on his own, we are given an initial and proleptic glimpse of the libidinal freedoms enabled by this short-lived period of unparented autonomy. A close-up shows us Joel's left hand pouring a measure of Chivas into a glass, and then his right hand sloppily filling the rest of the glass with the contents of a can of Coke. A TV dinner in a disposable aluminum tray is out of focus in the near background. Joel regards his dinner with a look of satisfaction, but his fork meets the apparently still frozen contents of the aluminum tray. In a gesture that descends directly from Chaplin, Joel picks up a frozen lozenge of what looks like roast beef and gravy—and begins to suck on it. The Chivas and Coke, the frozen TV dinner: These comestibles and Joel's awkward consumption of them help describe Joel's unsure embodiment of inexperienced not-quite-adulthood. Already, in this brief scene of dinner table insouciance, we can sense the transgressions to follow: the props tell us this. Next, another close-up shows us Joel's hands turning on his father's stereo, the use of which he has been sternly admonished against, while we hear him humming the opening piano chords of Bob Seger's "Old Time Rock and Roll," the actual sounds of which (cleverly mixed with the sounds of an audience cheering) take over the soundtrack as Joel switches the music on full blast. (The cheering seems to belong to the track itself, but, in fact, does not appear on the original recording. It assumes, therefore, an ambiguous reality.) Next, we are offered a long shot of the framed threshold that separates the Goodson's entry hall and stairwell from the living room, inside which the camera is positioned—almost exactly in the space occupied by the crystal egg. As the opening bars repeat again, Joel slides from screen left into the frame, into the proscenium made by threshold's architecture. His back is to us, to the camera, and his ass is arched up slightly. He slides into the shot, dressed in white socks and an Oxford cloth shirt, the tails of which just cover the protuberance of his buttocks. Only when he, in the next second, turns to face the camera, to face us, do we discern that he is also wearing white cotton briefs (whether Jockeys or Hanes, it is hard to tell). He is holding, in his right hand, one of the brass candlesticks last seen on the mantel, which he uses as a make-believe microphone as he aggressively begins to lip-sync the lyrics of Seger's fake nostalgic anti-disco hymn, while strutting his half-naked way into the living room and into film and cultural history. In a sense, it is not Joel who slides into the frame, nor is it Joel, his muscular thighs luminescent in the chiaroscuro lighting, who cock-walks his way into the living room. Rather, some strange alchemy occurs such that it is now Tom Cruise who enters this space. Innocence becomes experience through the virtuosity of a performance of ingenious onanistic self-enjoyment, in a closet karaoke performance made possible and, indeed, unforgettable, by the dexterity with which Joel/Cruise employs a candlestick to play-act the phony masculinity of Seger's overcompensatory manly lyrics and corny, white-man rhythm and blues.

As Joel/Cruise enters the living room, the film cuts to a medium close-up at his shoulder and then to a high-angle medium shot in which he approaches the mantel as we see the egg eerily spotlit and now only one candlestick—the other clearly in Joel/Cruise's grip. A few seconds later, Joel/Cruise turns to the camera, ditches the candlestick by hurling it onto one of the pair of matching chintz sofas, picks up the small shovel next to the fireplace, mounts the coffee table, rams the shovel's blade into his crotch and suggestively air guitars his way across the table top before jumping and landing on his knees, at which point the shovel becomes an imaginary microphone again. Next, he dispenses with the shovel in order to do a half split, then ricochet into a slightly perfunctory but nonetheless impressive (if only in its manic superfluity) shuffle backwards. He then flings himself back-first onto the sofa on screen left, and—in the grip of what seems like a masturbatory frenzy—kicks his legs in the air, high enough for us to see clearly the cleft of his ass, the indentation of which is indexed by the white cotton jersey that clings to the mounds of his buttocks. He then flips onto his stomach to dry-hump the cushions, his ass now luxuriously (if a bit too frenetically) on display for the high-angle camera.

To describe this scene in this detail (although, in fact, we have omitted any number of details that might have been noted) might seem, well, ridiculous. But it is worth our attention because it performs an apotheosis of the reciprocal condensation and consolidation of prop value and star power (itself a kind of value). This scene is, without a doubt, the most famous in Tom Cruise's entire filmography. (The most cursory search for "risky business dance scene" garners over six million hits.) It captures and foresees how Cruise's celebrity and star persona have been underwritten by his commitment to unembarrassed and reckless physicality. This is the star who eschews being supplanted by the stuntman, who continues, even past the age of sixty, to place his bare body before the camera's gaze. Although it is entirely possible that Cruise might have become the star that he is without having filmed this scene, his star persona is impossible to imagine without it. But given our concerns here, the scene is also impressive, indeed crucial, because of its deployment of and dependence on the prop. Because Cruise's performance is so kinetically charged, so manically uninhibited, one might nearly miss his agility with the candlestick and fireplace shovel and thus fail to register the essential role that these props play in grounding it. Cruise handles the props so adroitly, and with such *sprezzatura*, that we almost might miss them. Of course, the POV cinematography in the preceding scenes of parental admonishment has underlined their presence in the house as latent resources—symbolic, narrative, performative—to be, potentially, used up at some later point in the film. They are not, in Stern's sense, "histrionic" in themselves, but they give rise to and enable a performance that must be characterized as such.

This one-minute scene's furious density is also interesting in the way that it sutures itself to and elaborates the film's central preoccupations (Joel's coming of age, his reckless endangerment of his own person and his parents' possessions), but also segments itself from the larger narrative. It is a miniature music video made in the era of MTV's nascent arrival on the cultural scene. This scene is its own commodity, its allure constituted by Cruise's manipulation and creative "misuse" of commodities, and it serves to consolidate the commodity form of Cruise's star persona.[6] Cruise, then a nearly unknown performer who up until this point in his career was merely one among several post-adolescent newcomers in

early 1980s Hollywood, becomes a star through the labor of this scene, a scene in which he clasps props to his body, and ends up being clasped, irrevocably, to the history of cinema. The prop is a tool, a weapon with which Cruise dazzles an unsuspecting audience, but it also becomes a fastening device, a grommet that fixes Cruise's body to the body of film history and to the history of film performance. The scene is a dance of subjects and objects. The excessive POV-ness of the scenes that precede it, in which we are fictionally (however clumsily) in Joel's head, is exchanged for the dance scene's exhibition of Cruise as star, which is to say of Cruise as both subject (star as performer) and object (star as commodity).[7] Moreover, the scene becomes a segmented site of cultural fantasy that sustains itself through a cathexis (often mistaken) of this scene's and the larger film's props. One frequently asked question on the internet for devotees of this film runs something like: "Does Tom Cruise wear Ray Bans in the dance scene in *Risky Business*?" Answer: He does not. The Ray Ban

"Wayfarers," of course, are featured across the film, including in the first close-up of his face, just following the title sequence. Sales of Ray Ban Wayfarers shot up 2000% in the aftermath of the film's successful release. They became indelibly associated with the 1980s and its ascendant neoliberal values of ruthless upward mobility and carefree luxury expenditure. They became, in other words, one of the props of the decade's ideology, a periodizing marker of the Reagan era.[8]

6
Modalities of the Prop beyond the Studio

Props and their operations are woven into the fabric of the Hollywood mode of production and populate other traditions of filmmaking. Do prop operations in other cinematic modes articulate something of the prop's modality, something that is unique or distinct to these specific traditions? How is the prop put to use in art cinema, sex cinema, and the avant-garde film? The excursions below flesh out the potentials of thinking the prop through its iterative appearances and specificities, speculatively proposing some features of the prop's value to filmmaking styles and movements less reliant on capital-intensive studio production.

Art Cinema's Potato

A potato is an image of ubiquity. Ubiquity comes in its lumpen, knobby shape, its humble rootedness a picture of those modest things that cinematic illumination can only describe, but never wholly model out of its own plastic gaze. One can't peel or boil a potato-like object. The potato is a cheap, plentiful,

vegetal humility. It not only needs to be placed but also needs to be worked to appear not merely as background but as that suturing agent of propness, the prop that holds up, the prop that announces how it belongs to a cinematic world. Both plenitude and privation, sustenance and survival, the potato's figuration is also an announcement of the durative, of the temporalities that weave life as lived, labored, and routinized, as graspable units of activity that sew together the day. In this sense, the potato is an agent of cinematic time.

If the prop in part marks cinema's complex methods of crafting varieties of realism by constituting a plentiful world of thingly particularity, then one can point to varied objects that might instantiate cinematic verisimilitude and the work of its crafting. What might we understand of the prop from the vantage point of that lowly tuber, the cinematic potato? And how does art cinema harness the potato as prop, both in the sense of prop as material support and property of its fiction?

The potato occupies a privileged place in art history and particularly European painting, in which its location as the object of toil in agrarian, peasant life centers the frame of various elaborations of realist form from Jean-François Millet and Jules Bastien-Lepage to the post-Impressionist works of Vincent van Gogh. In painting, allied with the articulation of a lifeworld, a terrain of sweat and survival, the potato signals a humble mode of life, the material that provides the seedbed for subsistence. In cinema, no filmmaker is more ardent a devotee of the potato as object and ethos than Agnès Varda, who sees in the potato a world of gleaning and gathering in *The Gleaners and I* (2000), in which the practices of rescuing wasted potatoes elaborates a relationship to environmental sustenance. Varda's predilection for heart-shaped potatoes is emblematic for her search for humble variability and knobbled contingency.

As a cinematic prop, the potato troubles the bounds between gesture and object, process and thing—not unlike other props that are constituted by being handled and which necessitate their own on-screen transformation for their on-screen work. What we want to contend is that the potato has a very special significance due to its alignment with process, time, and endurance. Martin Brady suggests that the potato is broadly an object that bears a strong "resistance to metaphorization." For Brady, it holds interest by virtue of the nature of its necessity, its demanding and obdurate materiality, in that "it belongs to a minority of foodstuffs that are inedible, and thus nutritionally worthless, when raw. Rendering a potato edible through cooking is a transformation analogous (but not equivalent) to the construction of meaning or significance. Second, for all its ubiquity, in kitchens and cinemas, the potato is not—unlike, say, strawberries or rosemary—easily read symbolically."[1] The conversion of the potato into edibility, its processing into sustenance, and therefore human use as comestible starch, is also, as Brady suggests, a recomposition into the field of signification, but one within which it can appear only as itself.

It thus follows that in cinema, the potato, whole or peeled, prepared or not, gestures to the obduracy of the prop, its irreducibility to anything other than itself, its raw (even when cooked) material. The potato's enchainment to human labor and its source as stony generator of human life's ongoingness, its duration and endurance, represents an extreme pole of the prop's power of obstinate materiality. Of and from the soil and grounded by a horizontal literality that locates it in terms of its originating, subterranean earthiness, the potato's capacity for cinematic transcendence, or what Brady calls "metaphorization" or symbolization, is delimited by its incapacity to exceed itself. In contrast to the figurative flight of the Eisensteinian mechanical peacock, the enduring potato addresses a degree zero of the prop as material object.

The excess that appends to the potato is thus composed of the bodily movements that toil over and on it, the ministrations of actors who handle these modest vegetal things. The potato, peeled and picked, indexes the body's labors. It is medium and instrument of the body's lived time. In *Jeanne Dielman, 23, quai du Commerce 1080 Bruxelles* (1975) by Chantal Akerman and *The Turin Horse* (2011) by Béla Tarr and Agnes Hranitzky, the potato's qualitative opacity rests in its standing in for the dull and repetitive time of quotidian *durée*, a temporal rhythm organized by the routines of habit. Akerman's hyperrealist masterwork concerns the daily regimen of a widow who divides her day between mothering, routine social reproduction in household work, cooking, cleaning, and sex work (largely unseen) on the side. Yet the housework occupies the lion's share of the spectator's time of watching, as her tasks stretch out in their dutiful processual happening. Jeanne (Delphine Seyrig) breads cutlets, cleans the bathtub, makes coffee, and, yes, peels potatoes. Many of these activities are performed beginning to end for the camera. Lesley Stern suggests that in the film the matter and stuff of the everyday transforms, as "enchantment segues to accursedness" and "ontological equality collapses under the strain of repetition," but the "quotidian persists" in the persistence of things, that is, the props, of realism.[2]

Having burned the potatoes on day two, as her world begins to subtly unravel, Jeanne must begin again. As she peels two potatoes at the kitchen table, in frontal address to the camera, Jeanne's frontality announces itself equally as, on the one hand, demonstration, flat and pedagogical, and on the other a performative tussling with the material, with the potato's skin, which must be removed. She frustratingly pulls the knife over the skin, continually finding new spots that need to be removed. The knife is dull, unequal to the task. She cores out the potatoes' eyes, enervatingly bathing and soaking them, as they disappear, falling into the tub of water to her left. Brady suggests that Danièle Huillet disparagingly commented that it is clear from Seyrig's performance, indemnity exposed by detail, that the actor had no familiarity with peeling potatoes.[3] This comment raises the stakes of the lowly thing: The potato's obduracy provokes and catalyzes the problem of verisimilitude at the level of the body's theatrical skill, the actor's capacity to provide the illusion and thus instantiate expertise in gesture. The veracity of the potato's raw form challenges the actor's ability to perform, ironically in a film that delivers to the history of cinema its most searing indictments of cinematic presence as reproductive labor.

Perhaps this persistence can be allied with the paradoxically non-decomposable quality of decomposable objects in the cinema. The implicit temporality of organic matter, of matter that quickly decays and intersects with the time of the camera and filmstrip's durative technicity, points to the horizon of cinematic impermanence and immateriality both. In Tarr and Hranitzky's *The Turin Horse* potatoes, too, serve in another register as harbingers of a painterly universe in a historical elsewhere. They are also markers of cinematic time, perhaps Gilles Deleuze's "little time in a pure state," a surfeit of organic materiality which suggests ongoingness.[4] Here the labor of endurance and subsistence is also linked to a process in which potatoes are ruminatively boiled and eaten by a father and daughter, destitute farmers whose livelihood is questioned by elemental forces as their land is swept by an ominous and engulfing wind and an apocalyptically besetting darkness. Without a clear harvest or vocation, the two proceed through their days while observing the ravaging wind outside as a portent of doom, and the arrival of gypsies leads inexplicably to the loss of water from their well. They attempt to leave this blighted territory but without explication, return. These two figures face what seems to be an eventual extinction, etched in the remaining repetitions of their bare living.

The boiling and eating of the daily potato mark a time that cannot pass toward progress or eventfulness, while the father's incapacitated arm forces scenarios in which the potato must be undressed and pummeled by hand, while still hot. In base encounter with the potato's form, its processual role in this pair's minimal sustenance is by film's end whittled down to a state of starvation, as the lack of water forces the two to eat raw potatoes. Just as the titular horse has refused to move, the daughter refuses to eat. Here the potato elaborates a fate in its rawness, quasi-poisonous in its uncooked form, a terminality that constitutes the film's imaginary of the minimal conditions within which life can be reproduced or sustained. The potato's properties, available yet resistant to incorporation, speak to its status as a peculiar kernel of art cinema's necessary ambiguities and tussle with an experiential terrain. Art cinema's theory of the prop could begin here with the temporalities, at once geological, obstinate, and obdurate, that inhere in the potato.

The Skinflick's Prop

Linda Williams writes about how Eadweard Muybridge's motion studies in their investigation of bodily movement also signaled a surplus yoked to sexual difference. She traces how the prop appended and articulated the legibility of performed movement in these works. For Williams the addition of superfluous props like water jugs, veils, and cigarettes signals a symptomatic anxiety about woman as threat and lack that stands in contrast to the functionality of task-based labor in the studies of male bodies. Rather than tools or instruments that might articulate kinesis, sport, or muscular force, such as dumbbells, axes, saws, or swords, women's gestures are accompanied by props that emphasize a register of narrativity: baskets, basins, scarves, and objects that exceed the accentuation of pure labored motion. Williams writes:

> The props associated with women's bodies are never just devices to elicit movement; they are always something more, investing her body with an iconographic or even diegetic surplus of meaning. For example, when a woman lies down on a blanket placed on the ground in an activity that is identical to the series entitled '"Man Lying Down," she does not only lie down. She is provided with a narrative reason for lying down and the extra prop that goes with it: she lies down in order to read a newspaper. In other variations of lying down that have no male equivalent, the woman lies down in a hammock and, finally, in a bed complete with sheets and pillows.[5]

The prop here is an excess or plenitude for housing the woman's nude form, and it marks the excessive in what she describes as Muybridge's "gratuitous detail." Muybridge's prop anatomizes and appends itself to the feminine, rationalizes and smooths its potentially disruptive appearance. The prop is thus also a frame. Props here, in Williams's account, narrativize women's bodily movement as intrinsically gendered, harnessing that movement toward a diegetic rationalization and purposiveness. At this early moment of photographic representation, props serve to make the woman's body legible as a scene of fictionalization. When women appear together in the motion studies, their interactions are structured by erotic interchange. The prop's instrumentality inculcates and inscribes the emergence of cinematic mise-en-scène and the precepts of narrative design out of the spectacle of embodied motion, one to which the 1960s sexploitation film links up in its extension of a genealogy of sexualized posing.

The 1960s sex exploitation film, needing cinematic time to be filled by activity that is not yet sexual action, but performative eroticism, provided a historical stage for a return to the pose. What would it thus mean to take seriously all the bits and pieces of domestic, private life that get utilized, seen, picked up, fondled or that merely exist as silent decor in 1960s sex cinema? Ashtrays, caftans, lamps, shag rugs, gaudy wall art, and cocktail glasses seem mere adjuncts to the mode's "main event" of soft-core spectacle. Nevertheless, certain logics of labor and looking are made visible through the skinflick prop's materiality, its circulation, accumulation, and sheer contingency. As in other spheres, sometimes the adjunct is doing some heavy lifting.

Those residues of the lived-in world may sit at odds with how we have earlier discussed the defined practices of set dressing and production design in the Hollywood classical studio model. The plotted functionality and symbolic grandeur of the well-financed Hollywood film differs considerably from the formulaic and prosaic organization of sexploitation films. Made on minuscule budgets in several days' time, sexploitation films signaled a developing independent cinema on East and West Coasts, capitalizing on new obscenity codes that permitted the representation of female nudity.[6] These sex films relied on that which was most readily available and graspable by the skinflick camera—women's unclothed bodies most prominently, but also the bric-a-brac of domestic interiors, kitschy lower-middle-class decor that arrays the scene of women's productive and reproductive labor, like kitchens, bedrooms, living rooms, as well as offices, brothels, photo studios. These spaces of everyday iniquity, far afield from the glamor of the studios, provided grist for the mill of sexploitation's narratives of women's autonomy as desiring beings and laborers run amok.

Yet props do become central elements of the narrative propulsion in the skinflick, which draws on generic features of the action film and melodrama. One resonant example is the use of an ashtray in Doris Wishman's *Bad Girls Go to Hell* (1965), a film which concerns a woman, Meg (Gigi Darlene), who kills her rapist, and her flight from her suburban home to New York City to escape the police, as well as the burden of her shame. Meg's getaway hinges on the availability and mutability of an object the likes of which we frequently see in Wishman's mise-en-scène. Wishman often filmed in her own apartment in Queens, so in some of her films we see her own furniture and possessions restaged, masked by different upholstery or rearranged objects. The instrument of retaliation in *Bad Girls* is a piece of glazed midcentury pottery, which can't decide whether it is an ashtray or a bowl—one can imagine a grandmother using this for wrapped candy. As Meg fights back against her rapist, the building janitor, Wishman's camera momentarily reverses to the perspective of her attacker, as an impression of the bowl appears to obliterate the image in a whiteout, as if offering a mental image or visceral impression of the physical impact on its now dead subject. In the film's diagnosis and critique of women's life under capitalist patriarchy, Meg wields the very same materials which to some degree also oppress her, the scraps of her humdrum, betrothed suburban life, with a husband who prefers working on Saturday over her company. In prior scenes, Meg is seen languishing at home passing time, cleaning house, dressed in filigreed lace, looking out windows also dressed in filigreed curtains, trapped in the dull cycles of reproductive labor. The ashtray prop as a murder weapon converts an object of Meg's domestic banality into a blunt instrument that dialectically points to her bondage and temporary release. Props in Wishman's films expose the illusory promises that material culture poses for women seeking some semblance of fantasized or incipient liberation.

The sex film prop is thus tied to the articulation of performance, labor, class, and the problem of the sexploitation film's "weak narrativity." The mode's use of the prop aligns with the kinds of sliding axes of spectatorial attention to marginalia that inhere when watching low budget independent films. The sex films thus invite a distracted and wandering gaze preoccupied as much with the mood of the urban, lower-middle-class 1960s, replete with clinking whiskey tumblers, pullout sofas, organic shaped lamps, as with the torpor of narrative formulas tensed with extended longueurs of nudity or corporeal enervation.

Due to the state of obscenity law in the United States in the mid-1960s, sexploitation films, unlike their hard-core successors, frequently shunted explicit sexual activity offscreen, complicating an understanding of the balance in these films between sexual spectacle and narrative propulsion, creating scenarios in which waiting and straining to see are the crux of spectatorial activity. Joe Sarno's *The Swap and How They Make It* (1966) concerns the involvement of a number of bored suburban women in a swapping exchange in their Long Island enclave. One key element is the censorial use of the frame to designate offscreen space as the hot zone of sexual contact, which remains unseen. We are stationed to stare at a painting, a prop of the interstice, itself a witness to the action as well as a figuration for the concept of a view. Here the view itself becomes a placeholder, a mediator of the absent sex scene. The painting's thick surface, its dense brushstrokes and oily rendering of boat masts in a quasi-Impressionist style, buttresses the scene, as body parts, arms, heads, and legs, rise and fall, in and out of view. This image makes a prop of a double background and a doubled frame—the tacky painting and the film's frame. (One could argue that this object is not in itself a prop, but decor, and this is a place where the sex film unfixes the boundary between decor and prop, as one bleeds into another. The painting's instrumentality is in its performative labor in the scene, a diffusion of attention.)

Another kind of frame and handling of decor that converts a picture into propness occurs in Wishman's *Bad Girls*, when Meg, early in the film, rises out of bed and joins her husband in the shower. En route to the bathroom, she stretches, walks around naked, surveys her domestic space, and looks out the window, which frames her nakedness. She touches and makes a kissing gesture toward a framed picture of Keane-style wide-eyed cats, their resplendent kitschy cuteness a linkage with Meg's equanimity with her material domain, an association with feline likeness. As she and her husband shower, seen through a frosted glass door, the cats in the picture look back, seemingly knowingly, in cutaway. Meg's lingering look and touch animate the object, bestowing it with a value of vivacity. If Sarno's painting offers one kind of mute witnessing, serving as a placeholder or stand-in for a sex act that is not being made visible in the image, the cat picture, activated by

Meg's touch-kiss suggests a different kind of marking of that which lies beyond the frame—Meg's subjectivity and another world of desire beyond the walls of the home and beyond the heterosexual couple form.

The conditions of the sexploitation image's specific materiality arise from the relationship between the female body, oft thingly, fleshy fetish, and the filmic spaces' decors. The latter often act as metonymy or site of surplus meaning. They solicit an oscillating gaze that seeks sensory texture, over which erotic anticipation spreads itself like a viscous preserve. Describing the prop's meaning in terms of larger aesthetic design, and through the overt and more subtle zones of a film's meaning, Charles Tashiro describes these objects as "silent witnesses" to the filmic action/narration. In pursuing the implicit meaning of filmic design we can, he suggests, "consider pieces of design that might go unnoticed ... on their own, each object might resonate.... Just as workers may have talents and skills relevant to their employment, but integral to their lives, so too objects used for narrative cinema have existence on their own to which they return after a day's work on the set."[7] The object analogized as performance laborer, actor, wage worker: The prop returns to an object life that deploys another range of its qualities, that remains out of frame, even as it labors in the image to hold the space of the diegesis for a spectacle left offscreen.

Experimental Cinema and the Visionary Prop

Another mode of production that cannot function without recourse to the prop is avant-garde or experimental cinema. In Chapter 2 we considered the prop's radical centrality to the theory and practice of interwar (especially European) filmmaking and film theory, but the prop is also crucial to radical independent filmmakers, especially American independent filmmakers after World War II. This broad church of iconoclastic (and iconophilic) souls includes everyone from Maya Deren to Stan Brakhage to Kenneth Anger. Annette Michelson characterized this cinema in broad strokes as being "predicated on a negation, critical or apocalyptic, of the middle-class society that supported Hollywood, its aesthetic industry, and art."[8] The loose confederation of makers whose works constitute what is often called "the American avant-garde" share a desire to create a cinema that is both autonomous from "Hollywood" and autonomous in the broader sense: existing only for itself, outside the structures of capitalist exchange and the demands for narrative representation. Ironically, the avant-garde frequently seeks autonomy through that most heteronomous of forms, the prop.

We need only attend to the first images of the film that is widely regarded as having inaugurated the American avant-garde, Maya Deren and Alexander Hammid's *Meshes of the Afternoon* (1943). This film's truncated credit sequence declares the irony of where and when it was produced: "*Meshes of the Afternoon*, Hollywood, 1943." This bit of geographical information is a kind of trolling on the part of Deren and Hammid, given that their film, made for $274.90, was intended to be everything that the films made in the same town for much larger sums of money were not. And yet, as the film begins, we see a shot of what looks to be a concrete sidewalk, and no sooner have we begun to establish our bearings than a mannequin's arm, bearing in its hand a large paper flower, begins to extend itself into the image from the top of the frame, from somewhere offscreen, attached to what larger body we cannot guess. The hand deposits the large flower on the sidewalk and then, through a jump cut reminiscent of the trick films of Georges Méliès or Segundo de Chomón (master manipulators of props), simply disappears. The film has begun, and it has begun with a superfluity, perhaps even a redundancy of props. In this broad sense, it behaves precisely like the Hollywood films from which it means to distinguish itself. *Meshes'* play with seriality, its radical plasticity of space and time, the magic of Deren's body's multiplied appearance in the same frame—all these formal operations are welded to appearances of props. Flowers, keys, telephones, record players, knives, mirrors: These are the props that populate the film. When Deren, who acts in the role of the film's unnamed protagonist, interacts with and handles these items, she sets off a chain of formal experimentation. From the moment she first drops the key to her front door, to the sequence in which the same key magically transforms itself into a knife, and up until the film's last shot, the prop is woven into the fabric of Deren's and Hammid's lo-fi cinematic invention. It is precisely because the economic horizons of this film's mode of production were so strictly delimited that the props used in it assume their overwhelming importance. Here is Deren recounting how she decided on introducing the particular artificial flower that catalyzes the film's bizarre unspooling: "I needed a large flower because a large flower photographs better than a small flower. I needed an artificial flower because I had little money and was unable to buy a large fresh flower each day. Consequently, I went to the nearest five and ten and bought the largest flower in the store."[9] The prop is political economy, at the end of the day, Deren tells us.

We see this same set of issues in the filmmaking of Stan Brakhage, whose body of work is strongly associated with the human body (its interiority and exteriority) and with a radicalization of cinematic vision that outstrips the profilmic itself. What can props have to tell us in discussing the work of someone who frequently dispensed with shooting film as such and chose instead to paint directly onto the filmstrip? While we do not want to confuse matters too much, Brakhage's manhandling of the camera was crucial to his exploration of film's capacities:

> By deliberately spitting on the lens or wrecking its focal intention, one can achieve the early stages of impressionism. One can make the prima donna heavy in performance of image movement by speeding up the motor, or one can break up movement, in a way that approaches a more direct inspiration of contemporary human eye perceptibility of movement, by slowing the motion while recording the image. One may hand hold the camera and inherit worlds of space.[10]

Brakhage's set of DIY instructions here evokes for us an image of the camera as itself a prop. Apart from this potentially strained point (for which we beg forgiveness), some of Brakhage's most daring experiments with form involve a radical cathexis of what can only be called props. For example, *Mothlight* (1963) is the first of Brakhage's camera-less films. To produce it, Brakhage took clear tape and affixed directly to the filmstrip bits of grass, flowers, and husks of dead insects—the detritus and debris of the natural world. Film prints were then struck of this source "text," this archival spool of organic life and death. The resulting film collapses whatever distinction there is between realism and abstraction: We can see the actual stuff of the world right there on the screen, as if we were looking through a microscope at a furious parade of the world in miniature. But Brakhage arranged all these things—and why would we not call them props?—in careful patterns so that, when projected, abstract and rhythmic patterns emerge. In some passages there is a sense of strong verticality produced by blades of grass whose length is arranged to parallel the borders of the tape (and resulting film strip), while at other moments there is a nearly formless frenzy of matter. The film marks an important passage in Brakhage's work insofar as it suggests a frustration with photographed cinema and an orientation to a more explicit mode of non-representational abstraction. In one sense, *Mothlight* rivals *Window Water Baby Moving* (1959) in terms of its wild realism, its desire not merely to document but almost to merge itself with the world. But in another sense, the film's rendition of the recognizability of the world oscillates between "there it is!" and "what is that?" It shuttles back and forth between the most extravagant representationalism and a sovereign marking of representation's limits. This work is all made possible through the presence of the prop—the once living and now dead organic materials that Brakhage scooped up from the surface of the world and deposited, not in front of the camera, but on the surface of the film. Brakhage's *The Text of Light* (1974) performs yet another exercise in radical reduction as the road to complex abstraction: The entire film consists of Brakhage shooting through a glass ashtray that refracts light to produce a stunning array of purely abstract effects. But at the heart of this abstraction—this *withdrawal* from the figure, from representation, from realism—is the glass ashtray, an ordinary thing put to work for the filmmaker who wants to show us what cinematic properties the cinema possesses, and the wealth of props it has at its disposal.

Kenneth Anger's *Fireworks* (1947) is another example of a prop lending a title to the eponymous film. This homoerotic reverie makes good on the incendiary orgasm promised by the title: Toward the end we see a sailor with a roman candle extruding from the fly of his white trousers; the sailor lights it and rears back, letting the fireworks' explosions stand in for the money shot that cannot be pictured. (Despite this act of relative discretion, the film was nevertheless subject to censorship and seizure by the authorities.) *Fireworks* makes a number of hokey phallic jokes and does so, we sense, by making do with whatever Anger could get his hands on, quite probably from his family home, where he shot the film when he was purportedly seventeen years old during a weekend while his parents were away. (Clearly, we must see this film as the queer forerunner of *Risky Business*.) A shot early in the film shows a sleeping Anger (like Deren, he stars in an unnamed role in this, his first film) lying face up, his bare torso exposed, the lower half of his body covered by a sheet, under which seems to bulge an enormous tumescence. But the tone changes from smut to the Chaplin-esque when Anger reaches under the sheet to reveal a small "primitive" statue, whose height we had mistaken for a hard-on. Anger's cinema carries on this vulgar (in the best sense) play with the suggestiveness of props. *Scorpio Rising* (1964) and *Kustom Kar Kommandos* (1965) extend the literalizations of the prop's erotic promise. In *Scorpio*, as Little Peggy March's 1963 hit "Wind-Up Doll" occupies the soundtrack, we see one of bikers (who are the fetishistic objects of the film's ambivalent adoration) tinkering with the mechanical guts of his customized bike, winding its gear shaft. This imagery is intercut with close-ups of wind-up toy motorcycles moving in formation. While the form of the editing inherits something of Eisenstein's intellectual montage and its articulation *through* props, the contents of the shots and the sound-image relation are matters of almost pure redundancy. The central metaphor of the song finds perfect, literal correspondence in the footage of the human biker and the toy automata bikers. The effect is something similar to what we have described above in Eisenstein's Kerensky sequence: The song's metaphoricity (however clichéd and degraded) succumbs to the literal referentiality of the film's props—the big bikes that the big boys ride and the little ones they play with. A motorbike, it should go without saying, is nothing other than a prop for masculinity, in the way that the cock is a meager prop-like stand-in for the phallus. *Kustom Kar Kommandos* repeats *Scorpio*'s deployment of the prop as a literalizing force that nullifies the act of metaphorization. Here a hyper-customized car is fetishistically polished, buffed, and caressed with what looks like a white feather duster brandished with tender care by a boy in tight, crotch-hugging light-blue trousers, all while the Paris Sisters' cover of Bobby Darin's "Dream Lover" plays. There is almost nothing in this film but the prop—the image of the boy who so lovingly cares

for his car cannot quite compete with the numerous close-ups of the customized car's artisanal bricolage. It is a car made of the bits of many other cars, a prop made of many props, just as the film is itself made up of the drag racing customizing boy, his car, and the song, all of them species of found objects shellacked together and handed over to our visual delectation.

Coda
Golden Rain Tree

An attractive and well-dressed woman in her middle age is crossing her front yard while carrying a cardboard box of china tableware that her friend has driven over to return. The box seems heavy, and she has had to hold it for several minutes, while listening to her friend, who has harangued her into going on a date to the club that night with a mutual acquaintance. A man doing some work in her front yard notices her struggling with the box and offers to help. She accepts his offer, and both walk down a path that leads to a small patio along the side of her white frame colonial house. A yellow patio umbrella, fringed with white tassels, shelters a table that has been laid for lunch. A tree has been espaliered to grow against the house's white cladding. The height and length of its long, thin, fiercely pruned trunk and branches extend themselves in flat, lace-like abstraction. The man sets the box of china on an empty chair. The woman offers him some coffee. On the table, covered by a geometrically patterned gold and yellow tablecloth, are visible: a silver coffee service, gold-rimmed white china dinner plates, and side plates, silver flatware, empty crystal water goblets, serving bowls, and an arrangement of red and blue flowers. She hastens to expand her offer to include the lunch that her friend has just refused: "chicken and salad and some rolls." "Oh, just a roll and some coffee will do." She pours the coffee into a gold-rimmed white china cup sitting on a gold-rimmed saucer and hands it to him; he places it on the table. "Won't you sit down?" she asks. He murmurs acquiescent assent. She pours herself some coffee as he faintly seems to be just about to lower himself, but then balletically, in polite reciprocity, he pulls out her chair for her just as she begins to sit down. Seated, she places her coffee on the surface of the table. He takes a sip of coffee, and she offers him the platter of rolls, from which he takes—to her obvious satisfaction—not one, but two. She stirs her coffee while asking him if he will finish his work today or will need to return. He butters a roll and, in a just-articulate genteel grunt, cryptically replies "Probably will." She finishes stirring her coffee and places her spoon on the saucer while he takes a bite of his buttered roll. She sips her coffee. Meanwhile, their stilted exchange (lacking something of the fluidity of their physical interaction) continues. Their easy, unconsciously graceful manipulation of table things and comestibles contrasts subtly with the awkwardness of the words they exchange. She introduces herself by name, strangely belatedly, and he replies with his own. (Behind them, always, the flat espaliered tree.) The man answers the woman's questions—about his work, about gardening, about trees. Children are told not to talk with their mouths full, but the man manages to answer the woman without seeming rude, while chewing and swallowing his roll. He intones the names of the types of trees he grows. She asks whether she has any such trees. She doesn't, he tells her. "But you have some just as interesting," he reassures her, as he rises from the table and moves to a tree just nearby. He explains that this tree growing next to her house is a Koelreuteria. "In China, where it comes from, they call it the Golden Rain Tree." As he says this, he reaches into the tree's canopy of foliage, his left hand now brandishing a secateur, and clips a small branch from the tree, returns to his seat and offers it to the woman. "Beautiful, isn't it? They say it can only thrive near a home where there's love." She holds it admiringly and replies, "Beautiful legend." He murmurs in inarticulate agreement and then declares his need to return to work and thanks her for the coffee. She looks down at the cutting in her hands and then looks up after his retreating figure. The man has given her something that was already hers and has placed it in her hands. She has given him what was hers to give: an elegantly modest suburban repast and some of her time and attention. A cardboard box of china, rolls, coffee, a cutting from a Golden Rain Tree: these things have been passed from body to body, as words have passed from speaking mouth to listening ear. Each object has provided or occasioned a minor but nonetheless tangible shift in mood, proximity, and knowledge. Labor has been expended, labor has been paused, labor has been the object of conversation. Attention has been drawn to what was there all along. Backgrounds have become foregrounds, and the contours of a little world come into being.

Theses on the Prop

1. The possibility of fiction rests on the orchestration of signs, themselves signifiers of the real that support fiction's allusions to what exists. In literary fiction, these signifiers are words, weightless, but also weighed down by the duty to give weight to a world that does not exist, except in the fiction's parasitic portrayal of the world.
2. Cinema traffics not only in signs but also in the world itself. Cinema expropriates the world's objects as they are and makes of them (makes do with them) as it will and as it chooses. The world is cinema's prop-in-waiting.
3. The world lies in wait for the camera, although it does not know that it does so. The camera turns *the* world into *its* world, converts things as they were into things to be seen on-screen.
4. The world would seem to exist for cinema's use, and cinema makes use of the world, turning the world into a laboratory or playground of use.
5. Some things exist for themselves. A rock. A stone. A tree. Filmed, however, rocks and stones and trees assume another demeanor. Once silent, having been

filmed, they now ask a question: Of what use are we to this film?

6. By lending itself to film, the world becomes the film's prop. Film takes images of the world away from the world and stores them: It delaminates images of things from the things themselves. It turns being into having. What once belonged to itself now also belongs to the film.

7. Turning being into having is a harmless activity, in and of itself, perhaps. Making an image of a chair does not hurt the chair, the owner of the chair, or the person who made the chair. But the fact of film itself, the ease with which it turns things into images of themselves, suggests that at its heart, it at the very least embodies an ontological instrumentality in which everything that existed for itself begins, in being filmed, to exist for something or someone else.

8. A photograph of a chair does not seem to ask the same question that a filmed image of a chair asks. The photograph of a chair is that chair in an instant, as it was in that instant, and, yes, as it could be seen and imaged, but imaged so as to re-present it only as itself. This is a chair, the photograph says. This is another chair, another photograph says.

9. A chair in a film exists in a temporal duration. Shot of a room with a chair. Character A enters and sits on the chair. Having been sat on renders the chair as having been waiting to be sat on, and once sat on, it supports (props up) Character A, in both his bodily weight and materiality. It also supports him

(props him up) in whatever activity is required of him by the film and its narrative events. Something will happen to the chair on film even if no one sits in it: It becomes the chair that Character A did not sit on.

10. Cinematic narration, therefore—being a temporal art, technique, or activity—has something to do with instrumentality, and therefore with prop-making, or with the necessity of making props. For narrative to take place, it must take things and deploy them in the service of its own ends. Narrative's ontology could be said to be the mere fact of temporal duration, and therefore of some sort of change that is suffered, experienced, witnessed, endured. But that change can only be registered in the change in an object. Even this most minimal example of narration, "time passed," converts time, an abstraction, into, yes, a subject, but a subject with objective dimensions: Its property is *to pass*. Narrative drags everything down onto a horizontal axis: the axis on which things live and die, but, before that, the axis on which things become objects for subjects.

11. Time turns us all into things. Narrative cinema is the cinema of the prop.

12. Prop is short for property. Typically, a prop, whether in theater or cinema, is a movable object, transportable. In industrial filmmaking, the property department manages those movable objects that can be placed here or there. Insofar, however, as cinema turns everything into property by turning everything

into a moving image, the prop department is only a condensation of cinema's properties.
13. A prop-as-commodity's over-visibility brings back into view the invisible social relations that the commodity-as-commodity would rather keep hidden from sight. The badly functioning prop might also bring this labor process into view, just as when Marx reminds us that badly spun thread or a dull knife compels us to think of the workers who made these things.
14. The prop produces social knowledge. Madame Aubain's parlor in Flaubert's *A Simple Heart*: Objects ground the fiction, give its world a world (of things), make a world for the fiction out of the all-too-credible things of the world. This parlor's "eight mahogany chairs lined up against the white-painted wainscoting" tell us what kind of living room this is and what sort of woman Madame Aubain might be.
15. In Douglas Sirk's *There's Always Tomorrow* (1956) Clifford Groves (Fred McMurray) makes toys in a small toy workshop or factory of which he is the proprietor. One of the toys he has designed is Robbie the Robot. Robbie is a fake commodity that looks just like any number of other toy robots marketed to children in the 1950s. The prototypes for them that we see in Clifford's studio and factory showroom must either be commodities bought (perhaps modestly adapted or tweaked?) and inserted into the film. Or they might have been fabricated expressly for the needs of this film. We are looking,

therefore, at something like a prop department when looking at this image of the diegetic world. It does not surprise us that props, once cathected by our attention, return us to a consideration of mode of production. Because it begins with the vision of the toy factory and thus begins with a question of the fabrication of unnecessary objects that nonetheless seem necessary supports to the development of the human being, this film makes us especially aware of all the other props the film puts before us. Looked at from a certain perspective, the entire film seems an essay on or love letter to the prop. Looked at from a certain perspective, most films might seem the same.

16. Props are the toys of cinematic narration. They allow the narrative to grow, develop, mature. They also participate in the stupid obsolescence of toys. The narrative, having used the prop in order to develop a scene, may then cast it aside, just as a child discards or ignores a toy it no longer needs or in which it has no interest.

17. The extra is the human prop. The logic of the extra is that any one of them might step forward from the crowd and suddenly claim our attention. (Much of Hitchcock's work seems to issue from this possibility.) Next to or near the extra: the character actor, the type-cast actor. Many modalities of performance, in fact, border on the inorganic life of the prop. (Bresson called actors "models"; the same less-than-human condition was foreseen by Arnheim before him.)

18. The property department is the nonhuman casting department. Given the shuffling around, purchasing, purposing, and repurposing of things, the deployment of them for use, the enlisting of them for a performance of the world in which the things of the world make their appearances, is "property management" a better term for what happens on a movie set than "film production"?
19. The prop is the smallest unit by which to measure the cinema's possessive grasping at the world.
20. The cinema sits in the shadow of ownership cast by the prop.

Acknowledgments

For conversation, counsel, and solidarity while writing this book, we would like to thank the following: Mal Ahern, Erika Balsom, Jennifer Fay, Seb Franklin, Flavia Frigeri, Robert Gordon, Sofia Gotti, Manuele Gragnolati, Katherine Groo, Rhiannon Harries, Christoph Holzhey, Joanna Hogg, Mark Kermode, Michael Lawrence, Amanda Lillie, Matilde Nardelli, Jules O'Dwyer, Claudia Peppel, Brigitte Peucker, Alex Pickett, Brian Price, Alessandra Raengo, Martin Ruehl, Jocelyn Sczepaniak-Gillece, Sam Spike, Luke Syson, Amy Tobin, Filippo Trentin, Emma Widdis, Ben Wilck, Linda Ruth Williams, Emma Wilson, Charles Wolfe, and Genevieve Yue. Many thanks to Caetlin Benson-Allott and Jennifer Fay for their generous and helpful reviews, and to Thomas Lay and the Fordham University Press team for guiding the book into publication.

Notes

1. A Strand of Rope
1 André Bazin, "Theater and Cinema—Part Two," *What Is Cinema?*, vol. 1, ed. and trans. Hugh Gray (1967; Berkeley: University of California Press, 2005), 102–103.

2 Christian Metz, in his attempt to consider how the individual shot signifies, chooses a shot of what might be considered the ur-prop, the handgun: "A close-up of a revolver does not mean 'revolver' (a purely lexical unity), but at the very least, and without speaking of the connotations, it signifies 'Here is a revolver!'" ("The Cinema: Language or Language System?," in *Film Language: A Semiotics of the Cinema*, trans. Michael Taylor [Chicago: University of Chicago Press, 1974], 67). Metz's choice of examples is telling. He might have used a close-up of a human face or a human hand. But somehow the prop is apparently—and to use language we have already employed—closer to hand when posing the question of meaning and of narrativity in the cinema.

3 Pier Paolo Pasolini, "The 'Cinema of Poetry,'" *Heretical Empiricism*, ed. Louise K. Barnett.; trans. Louise K. Barnett and Ben Lawton (Bloomington: Indiana University Press, 1988), 167.

4 François Truffaut, *Hitchcock* (New York: Simon and Schuster, 1985), 179.

5 The film's form has been the most carefully parsed by D. A. Miller. See "Anal Rope," *Representations* 32 (Autumn 1990): 114–133.

6 Truffaut, 181.

7 Of course, just as crucial, the labor of the script and continuity editors, the lighting technicians, the sound engineers, the make-up department, etc. etc. Then, of course, there is the determining labor of the director, whose collaboration with and management of the

aforementioned cannot be underestimated or ignored (particularly when speaking of Hitchcock). But we beg the reader to let our distillation stand.

8 D. A. Miller's brilliant reading of the continuity "mistakes" in *Rope* provides ample evidence for the grounds of what we argue here. His reading, in fact, although it does not announce itself as such, is a reading of props. See *Hidden Hitchcock* (Chicago: University of Chicago Press, 2016), 55–92.

9 For a useful definition of "business" as it relates to characterization, see Ian Bernard, *Film and Television Acting: From Stage to Screen*, 2nd ed. (London: Routledge, 2016), 12.

10 Hitchcock speaking to François Truffaut, in *Hitchcock* (New York: Touchstone, 1983), 167.

11 D. A. Miller observes this. See *Hidden Hitchcock*, 74.

12 On the literal question of the manual, we refer readers to Brian Price's parsing of Bresson's hands: "The End of Transcendence, the Mourning of Crime: Bresson's Hands," *Studies in French Cinema* 2, no. 3 (2002): 127–134.

13 In contexts outside Hollywood, or outside the limits of the Hollywood mode of production as it functioned up until the 1960s, props might signal a condensation of particularity. The domestic interiors of Steven Spielberg's 1970s films, for instance, summon the chaos of what seem to be particular and particularly messy middle-class homes. But even here, the props' abundant particularity is actually a means of grounding the fictional in a generalized setting.

2. Reading for the Prop

1 Robert Bresson, *Notes on the Cinematographer*, trans. Jonathan Griffin (Los Angeles: Green Integer, 1997), 111.

2 Immanuel Kant, *Critique of the Power of Judgment*, trans. Paul Guyer and Eric Matthews (Cambridge: Cambridge University Press, 2000), 185.

3 Bresson, *Notes on the Cinematographer*, 32.

4 Bresson, *Notes on the Cinematographer*, 41.

5 Siegfried Kracauer, *Theory of Film: The Redemption of Physical Reality* (Princeton, NJ: Princeton University Press, 1997), 309; Lesley Stern, "'Paths that Wind through the Thicket of Things,'" *Critical Inquiry* 28, no. 1 (2001): 317–354.

6 See Bill Brown, *A Sense of Things: The Object Matter of American Literature* (Chicago: University of Chicago Press, 2003).

7 Volker Pantenburg, "The Cinematographic State of Things," in *Cinematographic Objects*, ed. Volker Pantenburg (Berlin: August Verlag, 2015), 11.

8 Martin Heidegger, "The Thing," *Poetry, Language, Thought*, trans. Albert Hofstadter (New York: Harper & Row, 1971), 165.

9 Heidegger, "The Thing," 165.

10 Heidegger, "The Thing," 174.

11 Stern, "'Paths That Wind through the Thicket of Things,'" 324.

12 Stern, "'Paths That Wind through the Thicket of Things,'" 325.

13 Jean Epstein, "On Certain Characteristics of *Photogénie*," in *French Film Theory & Criticism, 1907–1939*, vol. 1, ed. Richard Abel (Princeton, NJ: Princeton University Press, 1988), 317.

14 Jean Epstein, "The Cinema Seen from Etna," in *Jean Epstein: Critical Essays and New Translations*, ed. Jason Paul and Sarah Keller (Amsterdam: Amsterdam University Press, 2012), Keller and Paul, 289.

15 Christophe Wall-Romana, "Epstein's Photogénie as Corporeal Vision," in *Jean Epstein: Critical Essays and New Translations*, ed. Jason Paul and Sarah Keller, 54–55.

16 Jean Epstein, "For a New Avant-Garde," in *French Film Theory & Criticism, 1907–1939*, vol. 1, ed. Richard Abel, 352.

17 Pantenburg, *Cinematographic Objects: Things and Operations*, 11.

18 Louis Aragon, "On Decor," in *The Shadow and its Shadow: Surrealist Writings on the Cinema*, ed. and trans. Paul Hammond, 3rd ed. (San Francisco: City Lights Books, 2000), 51–52.

19 This litany is one that returns in a very different form, despite the disavowal of the aesthetic, in new materialist work such as Jane Bennett's *Vibrant Matter: A Political Ontology of Things* (Durham, NC: Duke University Press, 2010).

20 Aragon, "On Decor," 53.

21 Aragon, "On Decor," 53.

22 Francesco Casetti, "Objects on the Screen: Tools, Things, Events," in *Cinematographic Objects: Things and Operations*, ed. Volker Pantenburg, 26.

23 Viktor Shklovsky, "Art as Device," in *Theory of Prose*, trans. Benjamin Sher (1929; Elmwood Park, IL: Dalkey Archive Press, 1991), 6.

24 Kracauer, *Theory of Film*, 4.

25 Kracauer, *Theory of Film*, 41.

26 Kracauer, *Theory of Film*, 45. See also Kracauer's discussion of "the familiar," 54–57.

27 Kracauer, *Theory of Film*, 46.

28 Mary Ann Doane, "The Close-Up: Scale and Detail in Cinema," *differences: A Journal of Feminist Cultural Studies* 14, no. 3 (2003), 89.

29 Bazin, "The Virtues and Limitations of Montage," 46.

30 Bazin, "The Virtues and Limitations of Montage," 48.

31 Shklovsky, "Art as Device," 6.

3. Prop Value

1 Readers will not be mistaken in inferring our distance from the concerns of what has been termed "new materialism."

2 The implied, secondary discourse of such monstration is not, "Aha, a film is fake!" but rather, "Goodness, films are real!" They are real in the sense that they use up things (and use up people, capital, resources, both natural and synthetic).

3 Melvin M. Riddle, *Pen to Silversheet* (Los Angeles: Harvey White, 1922), 61.

4 Karl Marx, *Capital*, vol. 1, trans. Ben Fowkes (London: Penguin, 1990), 167.

5 Marx, *Capital*, 311. Marx goes on: "The mortal remains of machines, tools, workshops, etc., always continue to lead an existence distinct from that of the product they helped to turn out." The instrument of labor eventually transfers its exchange value to the product. "The lifetime of an instrument of labour is thus spent in the repetition of a greater or lesser number of similar operations. The instrument suffers the same fate as the man" (311).

6 Quoted in Julie Richard, "Shopping for Props," *Entertainment Industry Magazine*, November 1, 1986, 28.

7 Marx, *Capital*, 125.

8 Marx, *Capital*, 128.

9 Marx, *Capital*, 128.

10 Michael Heinrich, *An Introduction to the Three Volumes of Karl Marx's Capital*, trans. Alexander Locascio (New York: Monthly Review Press, 2004), 54.

11 An aside: *The Maltese Falcon* is but one of many films we might mention that are in effect "named after" the props at the center of their plots: *The Earrings of Madame de* . . . (Max Ophüls, 1953), *A Letter to Three Wives* (Joseph L. Mankiewicz, 1949), *The Locket* (John Brahm, 1946), *Blue Velvet* (David Lynch, 1986), *Lifeboat* (Alfred Hitchcock, 1944), *The Woman in the Window* (Fritz Lang, 1944), *Excalibur* (John Boorman, 1981), *Dude, Where's My Car?* (Danny Leiner, 2001), *American Pie* (Paul Weitz, 1999), *L'argent* (Robert Bresson, 1983)—to name a few.

12 See Vivian Sobchack, "Chasing the Maltese Falcon: The Fabrication of a Film Prop," *Journal of Visual Culture* 6, no. 2 (August 2007): 221–222. Sobchack's article is perhaps the most rigorous attempt to wrestle with the philosophical, material, and social and economic status of a film prop. It offered an example for us in the early stages of our research for this book.

13 See Bryan Burrough, "The Mystery of the Maltese Falcon, One of the Most Valuable Movie Props in History," *Vanity Fair* (online) February 19, 2016, https://www.vanityfair.com/hollywood/2016/02/mystery-of-the-maltese-falcon (last accessed November 26, 2022).

14 It could be objected that the ruby slippers are better classified as costume, but their afterlife (they are currently on display under glass at the Museum of the Academy of Motion Picture Arts and Sciences) seems to have turned them into something better thought of as a prop.

15 A finer parsing of these matters might consider the following: A prop purchased only for personal pleasure might be considered a form of nonproductive consumption; in this sense it functions in a precapitalist manner—exactly like, for instance, a relic that is purchased and

kept exclusively for devotional purposes and, thus, does not accrue any pecuniary benefit for the purchaser. A prop purchased, on the other hand, for a museum, for instance, that charges an entrance fee, could be understand as helping to generate surplus value through ticket sales. (We thank Seb Franklin for helping us think more carefully through these questions.)

16 Siegfried Kracauer, "Calico-World: The UFA City in Neubabelsberg," in *The Mass Ornament*, ed. and trans. Tom Levin (Cambridge, MA: Harvard University Press, 1995), 281.

17 Kracauer, "Calico-World," 285. Tom Levin has used "prop" to translate the German word "Attrappe," meaning dummy, or doll—a figurative prop, in other words.

18 Kracauer, "Calico-World," 282.

19 Kracauer, "Calico World," 283.

20 Kracauer, "Calico World," 283.

21 Kracauer, "Calico-World," 285.

22 Theodor Adorno, *Aesthetic Theory*, trans. R. Hullot-Kentor (Minneapolis: University of Minnesota Press, 1997), 21.

4. Realism, or the Prop's Thereness

1 Stanley Cavell, *The World Viewed*, enl. ed. (Cambridge, MA: Harvard University Press, 1979), 24.

2 Andrew Sofer, *The Stage Life of Props* (Ann Arbor: University of Michigan Press, 2003), 7.

3 Sofer, *The Stage Life of Props*, 18.

4 Sofer, *The Stage Life of Props*, 19.

5 Metz, *The Imaginary Signifier: Psychoanalysis and the Cinema,* trans. Celia Britton, Annwyl Williams, Ben Brewster, & Alfred Guzzetti. (Bloomington: Indiana University Press, 1982), 43.

6 Metz, *The Imaginary Signifier,* 43.

7 Metz, *The Imaginary Signifier*, 44.

8 Metz, *The Imaginary Signifier,* 44.

9 Metz, *The Imaginary Signifier,* 45.

10 This last sentence raises the question: What of CGI? Today the problem of such a Wellesian shot would be solved by the introduction of the digital special effect. We have persistently been asked the

question: "What can you say about the digital, given that now we don't really need props, thanks to its intervention?" One answer is a question: "Does the digital image exist so as to solve the problem of the prop?" Is the prop the shadow content of every digital image?

11 Roland Barthes, "The Reality Effect," in *The Rustle of Language*, trans. Richard Howard (Berkeley: University of California Press, 1989), 143.

12 Barthes, "The Reality Effect," 147.

13 It could be objected that some props enforce a regime of necessity: the overdetermined foregrounding of an object that we "just know" will matter later in some way, or the condensed symbolic value of an object (like the wind-up toy monkey we see at the beginning of *Rebel Without a Cause* ([Nicholas Ray, 1955]).

14 We recall our former teacher Richard Allen's excited instruction that Kerensky "walks right into the peacock's ass!"

15 Robert S. C. Gordon, *Bicycle Thieves* (Houndsmills, Basingstoke/London: Palgrave Macmillan/BFI, 2008), 38. Gordon devotes an entire chapter to the question of the bicycle (37–61). He compares its function to that of Hitchcock's MacGuffin, as well as to the eponymous statue in *The Maltese Falcon* (39).

16 Giuliana Minghelli, *Landscape and Memory in Post-Fascist Italian Film: Cinema Year Zero* (New York: Routledge, 2013), 103.

17 This was the very same year the popular front parties lost a historical election to a right-wing hegemon that would direct Italy's development across much of the second half of the twentieth century. The bicycle, Gordon explains, is "a piece of technology poised between the "pre-modern world of walking . . . and horse-drawn propulsion . . . and the speed-driven mechanics" of modern travel (*Bicycle Thieves*, 40–41). Gordon also mentions in a footnote that the bicycle is used in later films such as Wang Xiaoshang's *Beijing Bicycle* (2001) in homage to *Bicycle Thieves* (116n29). The bicycle's interstitiality, as an ambiguously modern piece of vehicular technology, is precisely why it lends itself so easily and interestingly to films produced in the "developing" world. Consider as well, for instance, Moshen Makhmalbaf's *The Cyclist* (1989).

18 André Bazin, "*Umberto D.:* A Great Work," in *What Is Cinema?* vol. 2, trans. and ed. Hugh Gray (Berkeley: University of California Press, 1971), 81.

19 Bazin, "*Umberto D.*: A Great work," 82.

20 Cesare Zavattini, "Some Ideas on the Cinema," in *Film: A Montage of Theories*, ed. Richard Dyer MacCann (New York: E. P. Dutton, 1966), 224. The essay was originally published in Italian in 1952, as the transcript of a recorded interview. It was subsequently published in *Sight and Sound* in October 1953.

21 Zavattini, "Some Ideas on the Cinema," 224–225.

22 De Sica quoted in Charles Leavitt IV, *Italian Neorealism: A Cultural History* (Toronto: University of Toronto Press, 2020), 87. Leavitt writes that "the *cronaca* can be said to define neorealism, however, it must also be said that the *cronaca* itself remains imperfectly defined" (87).

23 Leavitt, *Italian Neorealism*, 176. Leavitt reminds us of the myth (presumably true) that the producers tried to convince De Sica to cast Cary Grant in the role. De Sica resisted, but not without asking them to let him use Henry Fonda before he settled on Maggiorani.

24 Rachel Gabara, "'A Poetics of Refusal': Neorealism from Italy to Africa," in *Italian Neorealism and Global Cinema*, ed Laura E. Ruberto and Kristi M. Wilson (Detroit: Wayne State University Press, 2007), 187–188. Gabara's essay demonstrates the ways in which Italian neorealism travels to Africa by way of Latin America, through networks of professionals and film festivals. She also explores the way in which the term "neorealism" is nearly a term of abuse for some African filmmakers and film scholars. See 199–201. On the subject of Italian neorealism and African cinema, see also Sada Niang, "Neorealism and Nationalist Italian Cinema," in *Global Neorealism: The Transnational History of a Film Style*, ed. Saverio Giovacchini and Robert Sklar (Jackson: University Press of Mississippi, 2012), 194–208.

25 "La Noire de . . . ," *Presence Africaine* 1, no. 37 (1961): 90–102. Republished in Sembène's short story collection *Voltaique* in 1962.

26 Quoted in François Pfaff, *The Cinema of Ousmane Sembène: A Pioneer of African Film* (Westport, CT: Greenwood Press, 1984), 57.

27 Guy Hennebelle, "Ousmane Sembène: For Me the Cinema Is an Instrument of Political Action, but . . . ," in Annette Busch and Max Annas, *Ousmane Sembène: Interviews* (Jackson: University Press of Mississippi, 2008), 17.

5. The Prop and the Performer

1 V. I. Pudovkin, *Film Technique and Film Acting: The Cinema Writing of V. I. Pudovkin*, trans. Ivor Montagu (London: Vision Press, 1954), 115.

2 James Naremore, *Acting in the Cinema* (Berkeley: University of California Press, 1988), 33–38.

3 Noël Carroll, "Notes on the Sight Gag," in *Comedy/Cinema/Theory*, ed. Andrew Horton (Berkeley: University of California Press, 1991), 25–42.

4 A gloss of this exercise is provided in Edward Dwight Easty, *On Method Acting: The Classic Actor's Guide to the Stanislavsky Technique as Practiced at the Actors Studio* (New York: Ivy Books, 1981), 28–32. Stanislavsky's chapter "Concentration of Attention" might be Strasberg's precedent, as it focuses on the selective observation and description of objects as central to the actor's imaginative arsenal. Konstantin Stanislavsky, *An Actor Prepares*, trans. Elizabeth Reynolds Hapgood (1936; London: Bloomsbury, 2013), 63–82.

5 See, for example, Curtis Armstrong, "My Wild Summer with Tom Cruise: Women, Sean Penn, and the Making of 'Risky Business,'" *Hollywood Reporter*, June 21, 2017, https://www.hollywoodreporter.com/movies/movie-features/my-wild-summer-tom-cruise-women-sean-penn-making-risky-business-1014670 (last accessed July 28, 2022).

6 The scene might be compared to the one in *A Star Is Born* (George Cukor, 1954) in which Esther Blodgett/Vicki Lester, played by Judy Garland, performs for her husband (James Mason) a pastiche of the musical number she has been shooting on set all day. Garland makes use of a variety of household artifacts as substitute props for the props she would have been using on set. Jane Feuer calls this sort of musical performance a "bricolage number." See Feuer, *The Hollywood Musical*, 2nd ed. (Bloomington: Indiana University Press, 1993), 126. A close analysis of the scene can also be found in John David Rhodes, *Spectacle of Property: The House in American Film* (Minneapolis: University of Minnesota Press, 2017), 115–119.

7 For a perceptive reading of the film, one that touches on some of our concerns here, see Matthew Bernstein and David Pratt, "Comic Ambivalence in *Risky Business*," *Film Criticism* 9, no. 3 (Spring 1985): 33–43.

8 The Ray Bans and *Risky Business* itself were made to metonymize this period even, as well, by the opening *Saturday Night Live* skit in which Ron Reagan Jr. sends up the scene in a make-believe Oval Office. In this pastiche Ron Jr. does wear the Ray Bans, as if the skit could not do without the full array of the film's iconic signifiers in order to make its point. The question that apparently hangs over the appearance of the Ray Bans in the original scene in the film may spring from this widely disseminated skit.

6. Modalities of the Prop beyond the Studio

1 Martin Brady, "'Sich "bildsam" erhalten . . .': The complex ordinariness of culinary things in Beuys's *Gib mir Honig* and Handke's 'Warum eine Küche?'" *Modern Language Review* 111, no. 3 (2016): 798–799.

2 Lesley Stern, "Paths That Wind through the Thicket of Things,'" *Critical Inquiry* 28, no. 1 (2001): 331.

3 Brady, "'Sich "bildsam" erhalten . . . ,'" 797.

4 Gilles Deleuze, *Cinema 2: The Time-Image*, trans. Hugh Tomlinson and Robert Galeta (1989; London: Bloomsbury, 2013), 17.

5 Linda Williams, "Film Body: An Implantation of Perversions," in *Narrative /Apparatus/ Ideology*, ed. Philip Rosen (New York: Columbia University Press, 1986), 514.

6 For more on the history of this mode of production see Elena Gorfinkel, *Lewd Looks: American Sexploitation Cinema of the 1960s* (Minneapolis: University of Minnesota Press, 2017).

7 Charles Tashiro, *Pretty Pictures: Production Design and the History of Film* (Austin: University of Texas Press, 1998), 12.

8 Annette Michelson, "Film and the Radical Aspiration," in *Film Culture Reader*, ed. P. Adams Sitney (New York: Cooper Square Press, 2000), 416.

9 "Poetry and Motion Is Really Visual Bebop," *New York World-Telegram*, January 21, 1949.

10 Stan Brakhage "Camera Eye," in *Metaphors on Vision* (New York: Film Culture, 1963), np.

Figures

Page 2. *Rope* (Alfred Hitchcock, 1948)
Page 14. *La glace à trois faces* (Jean Epstein, 1927)
Page 33. *The Bad and the Beautiful* (Vincente Minnelli, 1952)
Page 54. *Citizen Kane* (Orson Welles, 1941)
Page 78. *La noire de . . .* (Ousmane Sembène, 1966)
Page 81. *Certain Women* (Kelly Reichardt, 2016)
Page 93. *Risky Business* (Paul Brickman, 1983)
Page 96. *The Turin Horse* (Béla Tarr and Ágnes Hranitzky, 2011)
Page 114. *Scorpio Rising* (Kenneth Anger, 1963)

Index

Adorno, Theodor, 52
Akerman, Chantal: *Jeanne Dielman, 23, quai du Commerce, 1080 Bruxelles* (1975), 18, 98–100
Anger, Kenneth, 108; *Fireworks*, 112–113; *Kustom Kar Kommandos*, 113–114; *Scorpio Rising*, 113
animism, 19, 21
anthropomorphism, 19, 25, 29
Aragon, Louis, 22–23
Arnheim, Rudolf, 123

Bad Girls Go to Hell (Doris Wishman), 104–105, 106–107
Balázs, Béla, 29
Barthes, Roland, 59
Bazin, André, 2–4, 29–30, 68
Bernhardt, Sarah, 55
Blair, Linda, 46
Blow Job (Andy Warhol), 61
Blue (Derek Jarman), 61
Brady, Martin, 97–98, 99
Brakhage, Stan, 108, 110–112; *Mothlight*, 110–111; *Text of Light, The*, 111–112; *Window Water Baby Moving*, 111
Brando, Marlon, 85
Bresson, Robert, 13–15, 19, 30, 123
Bicycle Thieves (Ladri di biciclette, Vittoria De Sica), 65–67, 70–71

Casetti, Francesco, 25
Cavell, Stanley, 53–54
Certain Women (Kelly Reichardt), 80–82

champagne (glasses, coupes), 10, 33–35, 41
Chaplin, Charles (Charlie), 18, 23, 83–85, 89, 112; *The Pawnshop* (1916), 83–85
Chomón, Segundo de, 109
close-up, 19, 20, 21, 28, 29, 31, 61, 62, 78, 88, 89, 90, 94. 113, 114
coffee cup, 60
coffee cup exercise, 85–86. *See also* Method, the
coffee grinding, 67–68
Collier, Constance, 10
contingency, 49, 59, 84, 103
Cruise, Tom, 86–94. See also *Risky Business*

Dall, John, 5
Darlene, Gigi, 104
décor, 2, 3, 11, 22, 23, 55, 63, 75, 87, 103, 106–107
Deleuze, Gilles, 100
Delluc, Louis, 22, 27
De Sica, Vittorio, 18, 65; *Bicycle Thieves* (1948), 65–67; *Umberto D.* (1952), 67–68
Diop, Mbissine Thérèse, 72, 74
Doane, Mary Ann, 28
Douglas, Kirk, 32, 34
Dulac, Germaine, 22

Eisenstein, Sergei, 62–64, 113
enchantment, 20, 23, 25, 29, 54, 99
Epstein, Jean, 18–22, 25, 28, 29, 64, 98, 113
Exorcist, The, 46–47
experimental cinema, 107–114
extra, 2, 17, 123
extraction, 31, 36, 41, 47, 75

fagginess: tacit, 11
Ferris Bueller's Day Off (John Hughes), 87
fetish, 47–48, 55, 62
Flaubert, Gustave, 124
Freud, Sigmund, 47–48

Game of Thrones (television series), 60
Garland, Judy, 46, 135n6
Gladstone, Lily, 80
Gordon, Robert, 66
Grahame, Gloria, 37
Granger, Farley, 5

Heidegger, Martin, 17
Hitchcock, Alfred, 123; *Rope*, 4–12, 58
Hogg, Joanna, 48; *Souvenir, The* (Parts I and II), 48
Huillet, Danièle, 99

instrumentality, 15, 26, 30, 56–57, 102, 106, 120, 121

Kant, Immanuel, 13
Keaton, Buster, 18
Kracauer, Siegfried, 15, 22, 26–28, 48–51

labor, 5, 7, 30–31, 34, 36, 37, 40, 41–43, 50, 51, 59, 60, 73, 74, 76, 77, 82, 93, 103, 107; hermeneutic labor, 79; reproductive labor, 68, 98–101, 105
Lady of the Lake (Robert Montgomery), 88
Lepage, Jules Bastien, 97

MacGuffin, 9
Maggiorani, Lamberto, 65, 70–71
magnification, 18, 26, 28, 64
Maltese Falcon, The (John Huston), 45–46, 133n15
Marx, Karl, 40–43; abstract labor, 43; commodity, 39, 40, 42–44, 52, 70, 75, 86, 92, 93, 122; constant capital, 41–42; exchange value, 36, 40, 41, 43, 44, 46, 47; use value, 24, 40, 43, 44, 46, 85
McLaughlin, Bill, 41
McMurray, Fred, 122
Méliès, Georges, 109
Meshes of the Afternoon (Maya Deren and Alexander Hammid), 108–110, 112
metaphor/metaphorization, 26, 61–63, 73, 84, 88, 98, 113

Method, the (acting technique), 82, 85–86
metonymy, 62, 107
Metz, Christian, 55–56, 60
Michelson, Annette, 108
Miller, D. A., 6, 127n5, 128n8, 128n11
Millet, Jean Francois, 97
Minghelli, Giuliana, 66
Minnelli, Vincente: *The Bad and the Beautiful*, 32–40, 44–45
Muybridge, Eadweard, 101–102

Naremore, James, 83, 85
narrativization, 3, 13, 44, 57, 58, 59, 61, 65, 72, 83, 102–103, 104–105, 121, 123; weak narrativity, 18, 105
neorealism, Italian, 64–72

October (Sergei Eisenstein), 62–64
On the Waterfront (Elia Kazan), 85
ordinariness, 28, 45, 65, 70, 81, 112
Ordinary People (Robert Redford), 87

Pantenburg, Volker, 16, 22
Pasolini, Pier Paolo, 4
Passion of Joan of Arc, The (Carl Theodor Dreyer), 61
peacock (mechanical), 62–63, 78
phallus, 112, 113
photogénie, 19, 28–29
Player, The (Robert Altman, 1992), 35
potato, 95–101
Poulenc, Francis, 10
Powell, Dick, 32
prop value, 40–52, 73, 82, 86, 91
Pudovkin, Vsevolod, 82

realism, 53–79, 86, 96, 99, 111, 112,
Red Balloon, The, (Albert Lamorisse), 30
Riddle, Melvin M., 40

Risky Business (Paul Brickman), 86–94, 112
Robbie the Robot, 122

Saint, Eva Marie, 85
Secret of Magic Island, The, (Jean Tourane), 30
Seger, Bob, 89
Sembène, Ousmane, 72, 74, 76; *Black Girl* (La noire de . . ., 1966), 72–77
sexploitation cinema, 103–107
Shklovsky, Viktor, 25, 30
Simple Heart, A, (Gustave Flaubert), 122
Singing in the Rain (Stanley Donen and Gene Kelly), 35
Sirk, Douglas: *There's Always Tomorrow*, 11, 124
Sobchack, Vivian, 45–46
Sofer, Andrew, 54–55
Stanislavsky, Konstantin, 85, 135n4
Stanwyck, Barbara, 83
Stella Dallas (King Vidor), 83
Stern, Lesley, 18–19, 24–25, 27, 84, 92, 99; histrionic propensity of things, 18, 27, 84, 92; quotidian dimension of things, 99
Stewart, James, 5
Stewart, Kristin, 80–82, 85
Strasberg, Lee, 85, 135n4. *See also* Method, the
Sullivan, Barry, 32
Sunset Boulevard (Billy Wilder), 35
Swap and How They Make It, The, (Joe Sarno), 105–106

Tashiro, Charles, 107
theater, 2, 3, 15, 53–56, 121
There's Always Tomorrow, (Douglas Sirk) 122
Three-Sided Mirror, The, (Jean Epstein), 20–22
Toland, Gregg, 59
Turin Horse, The, (Béla Tarr and Agnes Hranitzky), 98, 100–101
Turner, Lana, 32, 34

Van Gogh, Vincent, 97
Varda, Agnès: *The Gleaners and I* (2000), 97
Vertov, Dziga, 22

Wall-Romana, Christophe, 21
Welles, Orson: *Citizen Kane*, 32, 57–59, 64, 78; "Rosebud," 58, 78
Williams, Linda, 101–102

Zavattini, Cesare, 67, 68–70

Elena Gorfinkel is Reader in Film Studies at King's College London. She is the author of *Lewd Looks: American Sexploitation Cinema in the 1960s* (2017) and *Wanda* (2025).

John David Rhodes is Professor of Film Studies and Visual Culture at the University of Cambridge. He is the author of *Spectacle of Property: The House in American Film* (2017), *Meshes of the Afternoon* (2011), and *Stupendous, Miserable City: Pasolini's Rome* (2007).

SERIES EDITORS:
Erika Balsom (King's College London)
and **Genevieve Yue** (The New School)

Elena Gorfinkel, John David Rhodes, *The Prop*

Jules O'Dwyer, *Hotels*